WRITING As a
HEALING ART

WRITING As a HEALING ART

The Transforming Power of Self-Expression

LAURA CERWINSKE

A Perigee Book

A Perigee Book
Published by The Berkley Publishing Group
A division of Penguin Putnam Inc.
375 Hudson Street
New York, New York 10014

First edition: October 1999

Published simultaneously in Canada.

The Penguin Putnam Inc. World Wide Web site address is
http://www.penguinputnam.com

Cerwinske, Laura.
    Writing as a healing art : the transforming power of self-expression /
Laura Cerwinske.
        p.   cm.
    Includes index.
    ISBN 0-399-52542-4
    1. Creative writing—Therapeutic use.   I. Title.
RC489.W75C47   1999
615.8'515—dc21   99-39285
                                                                                                        CIP

Printed in the United States of America

10   9   8   7   6   5   4   3   2   1

Dedication

I OFFER THIS book as an honor to my beautiful parents, Evelyn and Bob Schwartz, who have always been as committed to learning as they have been to teaching; to my son, Jona, my greatest teacher of all; and, with deepest love to my brother and "sister," Richard and Ana-Maria Schwartz, who are among my greatest pillars of kindness and understanding.

I also dedicate this book to those others throughout my life who have taught me how to live by their example: my lifelong neighbor-parents, Dottie and Bill Hart and Zelda and Jimmy Hill, who raised me up and always remain close; my aunt and uncle, Muriel and Harold Solomon, who are models of indomitable spirit; my Aunt Barbara, who so freely expressed her pride in my accomplishments; Harry Warren, my beloved high school English teacher who still blesses me; my friend, the artist Richard Protovin, who taught me to see light; Maharaji, who gave me Knowledge; Maria McKenna, who sustained me in crisis and is a model of courage and grace; Frank Hatchett, dance teacher extraordinaire; Nick Mason, who taught me the universal dance; Alina Pantera, who showed me the shaman's way; and my godparents, Ernesto and Nidia Pichardo, who are ever a source of comfort and guidance.

Acknowledgments

MY DEEPEST THANKS to Mitchell Kaplan and Books and Books of Coral Gables who provided immeasurable support for my teaching and who have continually hosted the celebration of my books.

In memory of a loving champion and mentor, my dear friend Brendan Gill.

A salute to Susan Schulman, for finding me and for keeping me pointed in the right direction.

My gratitude to Michael Graves who lent me his wonderful house, filled with "writer's light," to use as my own private Yaddo.

Contents

The Key

THE HEALING POWER of *Writing As a Healing Art* derives purely from the conscious acts of observation and listening. The energy of these two actions generates subconscious shifts that restore physical, emotional, psychological and spiritual balance.

This process teaches effortless achievement as a key to well-being. It is concerned more with creating understanding than a particular outcome, more with recognizing meaning than discovering a "cure" or solution. By expanding our access to innate knowledge, the process allows us to surrender the need to fix, alter, or conquer.

Preface

*T*he only books that influence us are those for
which we are ready, and which have gone a little far-
ther down our particular path than we have yet got
ourselves.
—E. M. FORSTER

I AM A writer, artist, teacher, dancer, and student of
psychology and metaphysics. An insatiable communicator, I am
always seeking reflection—in language, imagery, and movement. I
thrive on creativity and exploration. I've built my life and my career
around these pursuits.

At the age of forty-five, however, after decades of prolific production, relentless financial struggle, and an exceptionally arduous single motherhood, my ambitions loomed tantalizingly near, but
perpetually out of reach. I found myself dispirited and debt-ridden,
frustrated and fatigued. Seeking comfort under a blanket of futility,
I took to bed.

Months later, I unintentionally found myself taking a course on
shamanism. A friend had shoved the money for the first class into
my fist and said, on the spur of the moment, "Go!" Long interested

in intuition and power—the foundation of shamanism—I enrolled. Only after I was completely won over by the teacher did I realize the twelve others in the class believed themselves to be taking a writing course.

The teacher—the shaman, to be precise—was an exquisitely literate and vivacious Cuban woman named Alina Pantera. She taught a stream-of-consciousness writing technique that was nondocumentary and far more focused, narrative, and exaggerated than the journal-type writing that many of the other students had, at one time or another, already practiced. Listening vaguely to her instructions, I rolled my eyes wearily, thinking, "It's no use," an expression that had become my mantra.

As a professional writer, I had already published a dozen books and hundreds of magazine articles. Writing had always come naturally and easily to me. Writing was how I made my living. Big deal—a writer. Writing meant hours at a desk, pain in my shoulders, paltry income, endless hustling, and relentless deadlines. The last thing I was interested in was a writing class.

"Write about 'It's no use,' " said Alina.

"Why bother?" I shrugged. "It's no use." And for the entire first year of her class, I refused to write. The day Alina said, "Your power is in your anger. Your anger is money in the bank. Your anger is your gold," was the day I started writing.

Anger was something I knew a lot about. And something I'd seldom been allowed to express. My mother, a virtual Doris Day full of smiling radiance and understanding, had raised me in the school of "If you don't have something good to say, don't say anything at all." And when I did manage to vent some venom, I'd be compared to my aunt, the one who was a walking reservoir of negativity and bias.

An intelligent woman with great wit, a green thumb, and an enormous love for animals, this aunt was also a devoted writer whose greatest dream in life was to publish her regrettably maudlin children's stories. Unhappily, she preferred venting her negativity to developing her social skills and, as a result, managed to alienate, at one time or another, just about every family member, neighbor, and friend who ever came near her. She also suffered from fatigue and an ongoing psychosomatic virus and lived an enormous amount of her time in bed.

The specter of being just like my aunt loomed heavily, and I spent a good deal of my life subconsciously resisting becoming her. But the truth was that I was a churning, burning cauldron of suppressed rage and paralyzing fatigue. Whereas my aunt was a noxious gas leak, I was a steam engine ready to derail in a toxic explosion. And like all good girls and boys who swallow their rage, I subconsciously drew exactly the people and circumstances into my life that would vicariously express it for me.

Anger = power? Anger = money in the bank? Anger = gold! Alina had snared my interest. The one thing I was more than willing to write about was rage. I wrote for days and weeks and months about chronic financial pressures, PMS, my son's temper, my perpetual edginess, my relentless annoyance with my mother, my guilt about my perpetual annoyance with my mother, more about money pressures, frustration with my publishers, exasperation with men, and on and on and on. A lifetime's worth of little girl/teenage girl/young woman/single mother's rage, fear, grief, need, desire, and confusion. No wonder I had been afraid to vent. Once started, I feared it would never stop.

So where did all this wallowing in the mire of a lifetime's emotion get me? Wouldn't I have been better off spending that energy putting on a sunny face, doing volunteer work, or just getting on with life?

The answer lies in two words: *truth* and *liberation*. The result is manifested in *healing* and *power*. The more I wrote out my suppressed feelings, the more I gained insight, detachment, and an increased sense of power over my life. I noticed that with the writing, I breathed deeper and was growing more aware of how the anger sabotaged my body. The more imagination I allowed to pour into the written scenarios, the stronger I felt. Eventually, the pervasiveness of my anger and confusion diminished, and I developed a clearer sense of direction in my life. My problems didn't necessarily disappear, but their hold on me diminished. I became more able to appreciate the privilege of my life and gained a more confident view of the future. My creativity flourished, and I was able to enjoy it in a way I'd never been able to before.

Writing As a Healing Art grew out of emotional struggle and creative inspiration. The Six Classic Principles of Transformation it comprises, which are by no means original to me, are fundamental to any number of artistic, healing, and spiritual practices. I have interpreted and integrated them from sources as seemingly divergent as Reichian therapy and traditional psychotherapy; the Wise Woman Tradition and Buddhism, Judaism, and Santeria; the Knowledge given by Maharaji and *A Course in Miracles;* architecture and the fine arts; dance and yoga.

The coalescence of these many and varied aspects of my learning occurred when I started teaching. As I taught what I formulated and practiced what I taught, I began to newly value the wealth of my knowledge. The more I articulated my understanding, the more creative I grew in expression. My intuition and my confidence in my perceptions sharpened. As I got stronger, my students got stronger. The more I witnessed their courage and felt the depth of their fears, the more courageous I had to grow.

It took years of teaching this writing process before I clearly grasped both the method and its power. The method is a perpetual work in progress, and I am continually refining and redefining it. The nature of the power is simple. It is at the essence of all art and at the foundation of every spiritual practice: Know the truth, and the truth will set you free.

Introduction

*T*houghts are locked in my head as in a beehive.

—MERET OPPENHEIM, artist

PROPHETS SPEAK OF the "still, small voice." Seers point to "the guiding light." Scientists acknowledge a primordial energy. Medical doctors know the healing power of will. All refer to an inner source wherein lie the answers to our individual quests. Writers create images with words. Artists bring meaning and sensation to images. Healers understand the value of the shadow—the darkness that holds the secret of transformation. All are alchemists—transformers, or in the context of *Writing As a Healing Art,* "trance formers." All derive their power from belief.

Humans, as conscious beings, are meant to live conscious lives, aware of our every feeling and response—whether painful or pleasurable, conventional or unconventional, pious or irreverent, constructive or destructive—uninhibited by the proscriptions of culture, religion, personal beliefs, or family values. We feel what we feel. Period. And that is neither good nor bad. How we respond to our feelings is another matter.

To retain or regain awareness of feeling is to develop power. To deny or bury feeling is to diminish power and choice: the choice of whether to act on a feeling or not, and if so, how.

The freedom to be conscious of our negative emotions without acting on them leads to a full emotional life, a fully present life, a healed and healthy life. We cannot be scared, angry, bored, or sad when we are living totally in the present. We are healed when we no longer hate or distrust what we feel.

Writing As a Healing Art expands our self-awareness and increases our ability to trust our feelings and live *fearlessly*. The process teaches us to recognize how the world mirrors our thoughts and beliefs. We learn what it is we truly want and gain the courage to ask for it, the power to manifest it, and the wholeness to maintain it.

This spontaneous approach to writing, which is distinct from traditional journal writing, opens doors to expression and contains energy leaks in the spirit and psyche. It intensifies our abilities to sense how and where our subconscious minds affect our physical bodies. With this awareness, we heal internally and externally.

Whereas psychology tends to focus on the questions of "why" and "how," *Writing As a Healing Art* applies the questions of classic storytelling: What happened? Where and when did it happen? Under what circumstances did it happen? It also asks: Where in my body do I harbor the memory? What is my pattern of response? What do I want the picture of my life to look like? What stands in the way of materializing it? Am I willing and ready for that manifestation? Am I willing to take total responsibility for my own power?

Personal power requires far more responsibility than is required to live in unquestioned accordance with cultural, religious, and family training. Therefore, it is one thing to say we desire more power in our lives and quite another to accept the changes that power will inevitably cause. Only we can determine the weight of history or the measure of responsibility we are willing to bear. At certain times, we simply may not have the strength to endure the pain of a particular recollection or discovery. Honoring our limits is one way of accepting responsibility for our power.

Resistance to acknowledging our own negativity and emotions often comes from our fear of their power. The more intensely we've kept negative thoughts and feelings under control, the more we are likely to fear that their exposure might obliterate our self-control, precipitating unstoppable rage, depression, or mania. We might well fear that our anguish will be unending or our pain will cause suffering to others. We might discover our inner resources to be inadequate—a terrible blow to the ego.

In truth, suppression of negative feelings provides only the illusion of control. When we freely express our thoughts, we are giving up the illusion and turning our anguish over to transformative power. When we acknowledge our passions and fears, we gain freedom from the physical, emotional, and spiritual tyranny of unhealed wounds.

Writing As a Healing Art is written for anyone with a need for physical or emotional healing, creative release, or spiritual exploration. Based on principles of creativity and metaphysics, the process teaches that restoration occurs *not* when we attempt to fix or change a situation but rather when we consciously and unjudgmentally observe it.

Writing As a Healing Art requires *no* writing experience or expertise. It is useful to anyone interested in developing writing fluidity, expanding creativity, or exploring their inner life. The process is also an excellent tool for those who wish to strengthen their communication skills or identify a new direction in their lives. Experienced writers find it valuable for taking their work deeper and making it more resonant. Its practice also allows us to more easily recognize inhibiting beliefs that stand in the way of reaching our goals.

Writing As a Healing Art is as effective for beginners as it is for experienced writers. It stimulates explorative thinking, free of boundaries. When we write in the undirected way the process prescribes, we find not the facts, but the fiction—the stories—that leads us to truth. Resonant truth. Truth verified by our bodies and manifested in greater health and fulfillment.

The writing examples included in this book come from my students, colleagues, and friends. They have been chosen for their honesty, strength, and clarity. In some cases, the raw truth of the writing may make readers uncomfortable. I advise you to remind yourself that the role of art—and healing—is to expand perception, regardless of whether it is disruptive or calming. Therefore, I urge you to consciously acknowledge to yourself the discomfort a thought or subject prompts before moving away from it. This simple awareness alone can bring about shifts in your perception and energy.

I salute all those who have allowed me to publish their private thoughts. And I wish for every reader of this book deepening faith and the courage to persevere. With the practice of this process, as with other artistic and spiritual paths, comes the joy of insight and the strength of inner healing.

With *Writing As a Healing Art* we learn that persistence on the path of self-exploration is a form of communion, that our devotion to that path is the art of healing, and that the role of Creator is ours.

Writing: River to the Subconscious

*A*n image that occurs in writing is closer to
the mystery of awareness than an image you actually
see with your eyes.

—DAVID PLANTE,

from *Conversations before the end of time*

> When I start an exercise, I never know where
> I will end up. It is as if I am guided by my pen,
> which has a mind of its own. While this experience
> can sometimes be frightening, at other times,
> it is totally exhilarating.
>
> —HORTENSE LEON, writing student

SOMETHING POTENT HAPPENS when we put pen to paper and allow the hand, rather than the head, to do our thinking. We gain an immediate intimacy with our thoughts along with a detachment not usually available through talking.

Writing, thinking, and talking do not process information in the same way and do not produce the same results. Undirected thinking and talking perpetuate our feelings because they further enroll us in our unconscious beliefs. Writing out feelings—in the free and exaggerated way this process teaches—perpetuates release because the writing stimulates awareness.

Materials

I feel a comfort, a relationship with the notebook. It
has become a trusted friend, a mirror, a story made
up of tiny details with epic proportions.

—MARIAN SNEIDER, L.C.S.W., writing student

WRITING DAILY IS fundamental to this process. A practical spiral-bound composition book or legal pad—something inexpensive, not precious, works best for me. Some students prefer something more special. Regardless of the form, the idea is to have no compunction about filling it up with mundanities. Many students find it valuable to return at other times to reread their writing about certain issues or periods. One student observed, "Since I often write when I'm feeling very emotional, rereading my writing at unemotional times is surprisingly inspiring. Sometimes it reminds me that I've known all along what to do, even though I've conveniently 'forgotten.'" For this reason, it's useful to write the beginning and ending dates on the cover of your notebook or folder. Post-it–type notes attached at the top of pages are useful as a simple index to important subjects, such as recurrent dreams or a particular issue or situation.

Many students ask about using a computer for this work. I recommend using only pen and paper for at least a year. The association between the hand and the page reinforces the neurological connection to the subconscious in a way that typing does not. Later, with greater fluidity and without the habit of qualifying thought, a keyboard can work.

Naturally, if writing by hand is an insurmountable obstacle to using this process, then by all means use a keyboard. However, since the idea or practice of handwriting is likely loaded with meaning for you, I would suggest immediately writing about writing by hand, like this student:

This writing makes my hand tired. All the small, little move-ments. This is not a big enough or fast enough form of communi-cation for me. I have always used a machine to catch my thoughts. I'm thinking faster than I can put the stuff down. It's slow. I miss out on half of what I'm thinking. It's not important enough to keep going on like this. I'm tired. I want to rest. Now the handwriting is getting sloppy and bigger. I don't care what comes out. When I let these muscles go, I'm messy and all over the place. What a weird sensation—my hand is only a part of me.

The Technique

The moving finger points and, having writ, moves on.

—OMAR KHAYYAM, *Rubaiyat of Omar Khayyam*

THE WRITING TECHNIQUE is very simple: Put your pen or pencil down on the page, start writing whatever first comes into your mind and keep writing continuously—without lifting your hand off the page—for at least five minutes or three full pages. By keeping your hand constantly moving, you allow whatever words or thoughts that flow into your mind to come out of your pen. These thoughts need make no sense or have any order. Your hand records what your mind would filter out, for the hand makes no distinction between speech and thought. What you say, what you think, and what you remember flow equally into your pen.

Do not edit your thoughts or search for the "right" word. Simply keep going. You are writing to lubricate the mechanism of self-communication. One student described how she "felt connected to others and connected to myself. I had nothing to prove or to hide. I was just there with my mysterious writing hand."

Spelling, punctuation, grammar, and handwriting (as long as it is decipherable) are irrelevant. The only requirement for this process is to keep your hand moving—even, or especially, when you think you have nothing to say. For example, write:

> I have nothing to say, nothing to write, my mind is blank, blah, blah, a blank, a blank. . . . I'm bored with this and don't want to go on. I wonder what Will is up to right now? Will! Why in hell am I thinking about him now, again, again, and again. Look how much of my mental time and energy he consumes. Do I think about him five times a day? Twenty-five? Is this still desire I'm feeling—or repressing, I guess—or is it more curiosity? And some concern? I really thought I was over this, this episode, this attitude, this presence of his in my mind, well, well, well. . . .

As long as you write with your hand rather than your head, you will, sooner or later, find yourself rafting the river of the subconscious, out of which revelations pour.

Write for at least five minutes daily. You can write quickly or leisurely, but you must write. You can write in the morning, afternoon, evening, or in the middle of the night, but you must write routinely. This process works like a mental cleansing of your psyche in much the way your daily physical eliminations cleanse your body. One student described:

> With my daily writing, I let whatever is in my brain at the moment come out all over the page—a surprisingly easy process which, nevertheless, I resisted for many years. As I write I am often surprised at the associations my unconscious makes, the memories that surface, unbidden; the imagery that jumps out at me, the words that seem to come from nowhere, and which don't always make sense. A string of associations and feelings floods my mind and actually keeps me company.

The writer Annie Dillard described in an article in the New York Times Book Review, the momentum of copious writing:

> The sensation of writing is the sensation of spinning, blinded by love and daring. It is the sensation of a stunt pilot's turning barrel rolls, or an inchworm's blind rearing from a stem in search of a route. At its worst, it feels like alligator wrestling. At its best, the sensation of writing is that of any unmerited grace. It is handed to you, but only if you look for it.
>
> It is like something you memorized once and forgot. Now it comes back and rips away your breath.
>
> Push it. Examine all things intensely and relentlessly.

Remember, you are not writing to create literature; build an archive; justify your existence; leave a memoir; or entertain, amuse, placate, or pacify an audience (although these often result). You are writing to expand your perspectives, to create openings in your life, to advance the action in your personal story, to glimpse a different picture of yourself. You are writing to gain power.

In addition to your daily writing, the exercises that follow throughout this book will provide you with immediate insight. Do them in the same way, with the same technique, you practice in your daily pages. I think it wise to do them in the same notebook and to date them. This makes it easy to return to an exercise and reflect on your thoughts and feelings of a particular time. Feel free to repeat an exercise whenever you need more clarity on its subject.

When an exercise asks for a list, write out each item in a complete sentence. This turns up the volume on your thoughts and, ultimately, allows you to hear yourself more readily.

Things I Am Trying Not to Think About

Assignment: Put your hand on the page, and without lifting it off or stopping to ponder, write a list of Five Things I Am Trying Not to Think About. Remember to make each a complete statement, a full sentence.

Example: I am trying not to think about Barbara, the bitch. I am trying not to think about the possibility that we have termites in the house. I am trying not to think about Mother in the nursing home. I am trying not to think about car payments. I am trying not to think about the dogs' getting out of the fence.

Review: How did the act of writing this list make you feel? Which item provoked the greatest sensation? Where in your body did you feel that sensation most?

Example: Thinking about Barbara made me feel a hardening around my heart, like a protest, like a horrible holding on to something. It made me not want to keep writing this list. My fingers cramp. My hand is already tired, and my handwriting looks like small, little left-brain movements. I want to get up and move my body. No more small muscle motions.

Assignment: Exaggerate the description of how you feel, magnifying every feeling to the point of tortuous melodrama. This is what's going on in your purely literal subconscious mind, so you might as well get it out on paper and see it.

Example: Thinking about Barbara made me feel AGAIN how hopelessly stuck I am on her. So stuck that if anyone looked for me, they would have a hard time finding me. My face is plastered so close up on her life that I can hardly breathe. My arms feel like they're holding hundred-pound weights, and I can't lift my body up to stand straight. My back is bending, aching, and pain is setting in on the joints. My feet—I can't pick them up. They are stuck inside concrete blocks which have been chained to her fence.

I don't even get to come inside anymore. I'm imprisoned out here with the dogs where I get to watch her laugh, and listen to her gossip about who did what and what they felt and why. It always makes me cringe to hear these stories— because I'm not a part of them. Now I feel even more stuck.

I am the victim! Don't look at me. My guts are choked up into my throat. My throat is parched. My eyes are wet. I want to run, but my feet are anchored. I try to move, but I fall over. My face hits the ground and scrapes my face. Good, I've given myself a real source of pain.

Assignment: Write about how much you *don't* want to write about the subject that most affected you.

Example: I don't even want to think about B anymore, let alone write about her. What do I keep this memory alive for? After all, all I want is to forget. I don't want to give these thoughts any import. I want to let go of this, let go of it NOW. I want to not have these thoughts dragging my heart down into my guts, cramping my fingers, and crushing me with their heaviness.

Review: What changes in perspective about this subject did you gain from writing? What changes in physical feeling did you experience?

Example: Until now I couldn't write about any of this. Of course what I really felt like doing was killing Barb, but I couldn't even pick up the pen to bludgeon her to death on paper. I can't imagine her dead. I don't want her dead. I couldn't let her leave me. If I killed her, I wouldn't be able to continue to drown in pain. Then I'd be able to mourn and let go—death can do that, I'm told.

Before I couldn't write, couldn't let myself go, couldn't attempt to heal. But that was then, and this is now. Now I am even writing in red—the color of blood. And I feel a sense of power returning to my arms and fingers. Is this the beginning of becoming unstuck?

Remember, there is no right or wrong, good or bad answer to any of these exercises. You are doing them simply to learn more about yourself.

Listening for Our Stories

I listened to him with the ears of my heart.

—JEAN COCTEAU ON PROUST

I hope you will go out and let stories happen to you,
and that you will work with them, water them with
your blood and ears and your laughter till they
bloom, till you yourself burst into bloom. Then you
will see what medicines they make, and where and
when to apply them. This is the work. The only work.

—CLARISSA PINKOLA ESTES,
Women Who Run with the Wolves

STORIES ARE MAGIC and medicine. They stimulate adrenaline and neutralize destructive energy. They have the power to comfort, heal, and transform. They invigorate the imagination and build spiritual muscle. They illuminate the path to the subconscious. The power of our stories launches us into galaxies of self-awareness.

In Western literature, traditional stories have a beginning, a middle, and an end. In the writing process used in this book, our stories can go on forever. They become vehicles for healing when we "lie with them," mulling them over, entertaining twists and turns, finding their sources, giving them new meanings, and enlarging their possibilities. As our awareness of our stories grows, healing occurs.

Modern psychology is based on the therapist's recognition of the stories taught to us by our parents, teachers, clergy, and peers and of their effects on us. Out of this tapestry of history and values, we began, as children, to weave our own story, subconsciously accepting certain threads we'd inherited and rejecting others. Eventually the stories we swallowed and digested began living in us, governing our emotions and choices. They became the stage for enacting our beliefs. The more we identified with our stories, the more power they gained to shape our view of reality. With this power we subconsciously enroll everyone we encounter into believing our stories just as we do.

Even Sigmund Freud likely recognized that what he was doing was very close to literature. He wrote, "Imaginative writers are valuable colleagues—[in] their knowledge of the human heart they are far ahead of (others) because they draw on sources not yet accessible to science. . . . With hardly an effort, creative writers . . . salvage from the whirlpool of their emotions the deepest truths, to which others have to force their way."

It makes no difference whether the story we tell ourselves or the world is "true" or not, healthy or unhealthy, constructive or destructive, tragic or romantic, debilitating or liberating; as long as we are unconsciously immersed in it, the story runs our lives. To whatever degree others' stories color our own, they too are running our lives.

The nature of the role in which we have cast ourselves is irrelevant. Regardless of whether we see ourselves as the good child, the happy wanderer, the loyal friend, the martyred parent, the hard worker, the heroic survivor, the perpetual victim, the die-hard rebel, the serious thinker, the devoted lover, the responsible citizen, or the free spirit, we have invested our role with tremendous power—the power to define us and guide us, the power to destroy us, and the power to heal us.

Self-Fulfilling Prophecies

Assignment: Describe another scenario from your list of Five *Things I Am Trying Not to Think About* with its most predictable ending, the one based on past history and your most disturbing expectations. Be sure to expand on the ending, enlarging its consequences and exaggerating the feelings it will cause you.

Review: Where in your body did you feel yourself responding? How much did your response escalate as you exaggerated the prospective ending? Did you feel more apprehensive or actually relieved after writing?

Assignment: Write the same scene with at least two entirely different endings—one for yourself and another for each of the other people involved in the situation.

Review: Did articulating the possibility of a different ending give you a different perspective on your situation? How did your body respond to these new scenarios—in physical location and in degree?

Writing Is a Bridge to the Imagination

The imagination is grounded in the energy of the
organs of the body, which is to say it has a
biological source.

—JOSEPH CAMPBELL

SCIENTIFIC, LOGICAL, LINEAR, or left-brain thinking, which is based on the objective weighing of fact and detail, calls on a mode of seeing without imagination. Myth, on the other hand, which is nonliteral, nonlogical, and imbued with imaginary color, texture, and detail, cannot fully be understood without entering into a right-brain or metaphysical state of mind.

The subconscious mind is purely literal. It stands ready to follow the orders our conscious mind sends it, regardless of their degree of emotion or veracity. For example, the subconscious perceives no distinction between jealous rage and simple doubt; both represent equal commands to annihilate.

We fear uncensored, wholly passionate expression when we subconsciously believe it will either irreparably disrupt our lives or bring harm to the object of our thoughts. We also resist writing out our raw feelings for fear of seeing them recorded in black and white. The very thought of making intense emotion—or even minor anxiety—concrete can easily deter us. Yet only the safe acknowledgment of our most repressed or unacceptable thoughts will free them from the subconscious and drain them of their power. When we write in the undirected way (i.e., the explorative process) that this book teaches, we find not the facts, but the fiction—the stories—that lead us to the truth.

The Most Important Things I Want People to Think About Me

Assignment: Without thinking, write a list of the first five things that come to your mind when completing a sentence that begins "The most important things I want people to think about me are . . . "

Example: The most important things I want people to think about me are that I am compassionate, that I am capable, that I am caring, that I am tolerant, that I am hardworking.

Review: Look at the list. With each item, ask yourself and write a response to these questions:

• When did this first begin to matter to me?

• Was this more important to my mother or my father?

• Who embodies this in my life now?

Example: My first memory of compassion? It was the guilt and shame from crushing little, tiny red bugs on the cement outside the house in Pittsfield. This was my big secret—I was a monster! Not compassionate at all. Not like the good little girl I was taught to be.

By whom? Who was this most important to? Mother was famous for her compassion. It was always open house to the world at our home. When were we only five at dinner? There were always travelers, diplomats, friends, students, other world-savers, or their kids, from everywhere on the map. Sometimes we had to step over bodies in the morning. And she was always caring for others professionally—and good at it. But not much actual emotional contact with *us,* I'm sorry to say. Or Dad, either. He was too busy traveling around, staying at other people's houses, eating with other people's kids. But compassion was important to both of them.

Assignment: Write a scene in which you have been stripped of this quality and totally misjudged. It has made headline news, and all the world knows. Make yourself your own nemesis and hold back nothing! Remember, this is fiction. You can make this as grotesque as a fairy tale or as sadistic as a Road Runner cartoon.

Example: What if my compassion is totally bogus? OK then, I am totally self involved and have no compassion for anyone or anything and everyone knows it. Once and for all.

Kill the red bugs! Kill them just for the pleasure of watching them disappear into the holes in the cement in the hot sun. They vanish, just like my compassion did. No more "walking in another man's shoes." From now on, everything will be MY way. GET OUT OF MY WAY! You don't matter! You don't exist! And even if you do, who cares? Not me!

I annihilate you with my dispassion. What is that condition called? It's a "disorder" and has a name. When you can't relate at all to anyone else's feelings. When you're totally alone. Finally! The solitude I've been looking for!

Don't bother me! I'll just stay home and read. You can't share with me, either. It's all mine, and I don't give a fig!

Review: How did this writing make you feel—relieved or agitated? Did any particular part of your body react as you were writing? Are you surprised at how deeply you knew this character? Are you more comfortable or less comfortable with your nemesis than you were before you wrote? What other mental, physical, or emotional reactions did you have? What was the most surprising result of this writing?

Example: At first I felt numb. Now, a shakiness of my skin. Could be the air conditioning in here. Now a tingling on my arms just under the surface. Something is making my skin crawl. Not like worms in a grave, but like Elmer's glue being peeled off the skin, but underneath. If I let it persist, it will tear my skin away from my body like in a horror film. I'll be exposed. I am afraid of falling apart. I have never thought of myself as afraid to let go, afraid of loss of control, but anything's possible.

The most surprising result of this writing is the violence and ugliness that comes out, and this ability to exaggerate physical feelings until they actually blossom into something new, revealing the violence.

———————

As you do this work, you will find that not only is writing a bridge to your imagination but that your imagination, in turn, is the bridge to your fulfillment. Transformation requires a merging or dissolution into a larger, more encompassing identity than that of the ego. The more liberated your imagination, the greater capacity you gain to integrate joy and satisfaction into your life.

Resistance Is Not a Failure

It is ironic that I often avoid writing my daily pages. Maybe it's because I am afraid of what I have to say, afraid of seeing those feelings naked on the page, so stark, so glaring. Yet, when I do write, I almost always feel some kind of relief, even if it is only the relief of evacuation. Nothing gets solved. Nothing changes. But it is a matter of bearing witness, of being alive. I write, therefore I am.

—HORTENSE LEON, writing student

RESISTANCE TO WRITING is natural, especially when it involves difficult feelings. Understand that resistance emanates from judgment—of others and of ourselves. All judgment, implicit or explicit and regardless of degree, halts the evolution of thought, feeling, and motion. It freezes growth in relationships and in creativity. When observed consciously, however, resistance becomes dynamic and can work *for* us. The moment we acknowledge our resistance, it becomes a motivating force and inevitably stimulates change.

There are times when we feel simply unprepared to take on a particular subject. This is not a failure; it is a recognition. Heed this awareness—and write about the resistance. "It is a piece of cake to write about my past," wrote a student, "my memories, my thoughts of pleasure, my things and people, my places. A simple word brings forth forgotten pictures in my mind. But then I hit a snag . . . and the material unravels. A spot that had a ragged tear. The tear becomes my tears. The easy, pleasant task becomes painful. . . . I don't want to write anymore."

Instead of fleeing from a painful subject or forcing ourselves either to look at or away from it, we learn to see how our resistance is protecting us. It is teaching us to trust our hands, minds, and bodies to tell us when we are ready for a particular exploration. One student wrote of her resistance:

> I don't want to go farther. This is as much as I want to know. I've learned about all I can stand. One day at lunch I wrote about my desire for revenge. My keen understanding of the whole gamut of torture and suffering propelled me on for pages.
>
> I was frightened. I was even more frightened at how elated I was to express all this. So, like a dog with a tasty bone and absolutely no appetite, I'd like to bury this aspect very, very deep where no one will find it. I truly want to bury it so deep that I'll forget where it is.
>
> This troubles me. I would have sworn that my inner core was the sunbeam I was taught about in church. It is not. Having unplugged the gate of hell, I got a peek that there is a whole crowd down there clamoring to climb out through my pen. Bad pen! Bad pen!

The Worst Thing I Could Find Out About Myself

Assignment: Quickly and without picking up your hand from the page, write a scene in which you recognize or discover the worst thing you could possibly learn about yourself. What is it? Who else knows? What are the consequences? How long have you resisted this knowledge? How much are you resisting this exercise?

Example: The worst thing I could find out about myself is that I have already grown old. The realization would come when I am out in the boat. I lean over and study the reflection of my face, given back without comment by the ocean, and my sense of bliss, connectedness, completeness is eclipsed as if huge storm clouds had blackened the sun.

Suddenly I see the lines of my face, the salt and pepper hair, the tiredness in my eyes like roadmaps leading back through my life without meaning, purpose, or lesson. Worst of all, the tracks in my face tell nothing of the future, belie no direction.

Finding no purpose in my features, I suddenly feel far from land, far from people, and seriously at risk of drowning.

I have to grope through recent recollections to find some short-term purpose (long-term purpose having failed). I pretend to be content to have executed another day and to have planned, in exquisite detail, the murder of the next.

This enables me to see some resolve in my reflection, and I start to paddle back to shore. But as I turn back, I realize that all around me it's grown cold and dark.

The more we recognize and honor our resistance, the sooner we are able to approach what lies uncomfortable and unresolved in our minds. It makes no difference whether our resistance is to a seemingly minor subject (e.g., hating to talk on the phone) or to an over-whelmingly major one (e.g., experiencing denial over a critical diagnosis). Once we honor our resistance, we can begin to grasp all that lies beyond it.

Gathering Vocabulary

> There's a real confusion between a thing and the
> word for the thing. But then I'm interested
> in that confusion.
>
> —CLAUS OLDENBURG, artist

EXPRESSION BEGINS WITH vocabulary. The specific words we use define our feelings and shape their interpretation. The more aligned our verbal vocabulary is with the range and nuance of our inner responses, the more effective our writing becomes.

The vocabulary that comes spontaneously through our hands to the page leads our attention to metaphors that dramatize the subject or mood of our thoughts. In fact, a strong metaphor—or concrete image—can conjure a whole world of feeling in merely a word. Consider, for example, the emotional weight of the simple sentence "My life is a sinkhole."

Metaphors flow readily when we are sensitive to our bodies. One student, in writing of her debilitating episodes of PMS continually referred to the way her "ovaries feel like iron fists." She pursued the metaphor, determined to find the source of her dis-ease, and eventually learned through her writing that she had been sexually assaulted as a small child. Her very sexuality was replaying the assault each month to reawaken her memory of the trauma she had buried too deeply to consciously recall. Not even years of therapy had brought her close to the recollection. Once she recognized her body's message, however, the symptoms steadily diminished and eventually disappeared, leaving her free to menstruate without suffering and to experience sex fully—the very things her subconscious had prevented her from before.

As another example, consider the effect of the militant vocabulary expressed by one writer: "I feel bombarded by his attentions. He will annihilate me with desire. Do I retaliate or surrender?" The writer obviously felt beseiged by her lover but was unaware of it until she began writing and examined her vocabulary.

Listen for the suffocation expressed in this description of a father's "nurturing" of his daughter: "We swaddled her with our guidance, coddled her ambitions. We were waiting for evidence of maturity before we allowed her out of our embrace."

Sometimes vocabulary from an entirely different context will enrich expression. For example, my grandmother once referred to her fellow residents at a retirement hotel as the "inmates" of the hotel. With that one word she completely expressed her feelings about her forced retirement.

Because I am an artist as well as a writer, the visual vocabulary of my art work often reiterates the verbal vocabulary of my writing and vice versa. My visual vocabulary became clear to me after an intensive period of making sculpture. After amassing a huge number of found objects and other elements, I began to see the common qualities that commanded my eye: objects made from brass, iron, and steel; rusted and distressed surfaces; blood, hair, and bones; baroque picture frames; antique gold, silver, and pearl jewelry; fake and precious stones; glass and ceramic shards; large palm husks and deep pile fabrics; boxes, bowls, and vessels.

Heavily ornamented and purposefully evocative, my work is rooted in the history of religious art and spiritual expression. Its style of imagery draws heavily from Christian iconography, medieval manuscript illumination, and Catholic folk art. The images often allude in composition to the Byzantine in their animation, horror vacui (fear of empty space), and delight in violating the frame.

The more I worked, the clearer the "meaning" of my visual

vocabulary became: The blood derived from the goddess cultures, the fragments and shards from Roman and Byzantine mosaics, the hair and bones from the Christian reliquary. I saw how my work reiterated the jeweled encrustations of the Carolingians, the roses of Renaissance painting, the nails of Spanish gothic, and the abundant vessels of Buddhist and African Caribbean obeisance.

During a time of deep emotional "excavation," I found the words bones and shards appearing as frequently in my writing as they did in my artwork. They were expressing the evidence of my "internal archaeology," of my determined digging into the dark mystery of my subconscious. Exactly this type of reiteration (verbal to visual and visual to verbal) occurs over and over until I eventually see or hear what my subconscious is expressing.

The image of bones expressed for another student her feelings of abandonment and inertia:

Nothing but bones is left of me in this desert, this emotional, lifeless desert where I was abandoned.

Vultures hover. So close I hear their wings. They are after something, zeroing in on some prey. What is it? What could possibly still be alive in this godforsaken place?

Let me get closer. Oh, my God, I can't believe what I'm seeing—it looks like a woman. No, it's just pieces of jeans and shirt. Stands of hair . . . and bones. The vultures are circling for the last pieces of decaying flesh off these bones. Bugs are feasting on the rest. Who allowed this to happen!

Oh no. My God, it can't be. . . . It's me. Those are MY bones!

Everyone, everything has taken a piece of me. Even though I was abandoned here in this desert, I still gave to everyone. Why do they have to skin me alive? Bones . . . broken bones. Doesn't this equate with death? Is this what I've allowed?

How can I reclaim these bones? They are in pieces . . . broken, shattered, disintegrating. Thrown out on the desert to dete-

riorate and blow in the wind to nowhere. That's where I am.
Nowhere. That's where I have been. Nowhere. That's where I'm
going. Nowhere.

Who took my life from me? A thoughtless son, an absent
father, a complacent husband, a mother and step-father who live
in their own world except when they need my help. And then, of
course, there's me.

The word bone appeared in an entirely different context in the
writing of a student who juxtaposed a sinister connotation with a
"beloved dog" association:

It's Only Poultry

This is it! I've had enough of this lack of love. You unlove me!
I hate you! I said I would cook . . . well, guess what? I've never
cooked in fifty-five years, and I'm going to mix chicken liver with
pork and chicken bones, and we will feast on the dance of a cannibal. In the candlelight, I'll watch the bones piercing your
throat. No, you won't swallow this one? Come on . . . a little bit
more. . . . One more try. It's only poultry.

This is my first cooking lesson. If you think I'm poisoning us,
it's only because you are a paranoid schizophrenic. Not a friend.
Not a mother. Not a partner. Not a fan.

You're a miserable piece of meat for a cannibal like me! I cook
and I eat your flesh. I'll boil your bones for my dish!

You unlove me, and I cancel our plans. I call you at midnight
to tell you I never want to see you again. Don't expect to hear
from me, I say. Are you going to be OK? I say. And you say,
"Don't worry about me. Worry about yourself!" And you're right!
Now I fucking worry a lot about myself.

I'm in the hotel, alone. I'm afraid of the serial killers. They could come in from the streets, outside, or from a room. "Any room would do," H. would say. I'm cold.

The manager resigned. It means prospectively a big mess. I don't know if I can hold on to the job. I have to stop thinking I'm going to work here for the rest of my life. Only temporary. Temporary job. Temporary love.

So I worry, yeah! I'm alone, I'm cold, needy, lonely. A child. You love me and unlove me. You're so consistent in the latter. I need a love fix. Can't have it right now. I'm at work. Tomorrow we'll have dinner. I'll cook my bones instead of yours. How's that?

It's eight o'clock in the morning, finally. I rang your bell this morning. I handed you two croissants. You thought I bought them. I only stole them from the hotel. I fell asleep in your arms. I just wanted you to love me like you love your dog. "Boodie, Boodie, Boo!" I tried to talk. Thank God I was too sleepy to say a word. You were holding me tight. The bone has dissolved in the acid broth of love.

First Sex

Assignment: **Part 1.** Describe your first sexual or near-sexual experience. Write just the facts. No description or metaphor. Make it as dry and terse as you can.

Example: She walked into my dorm room. She took off her shirt and looked at me. I looked down. Nothing came up. We lay down. She lay back with me on top. She was matter of fact. I was anxiety ridden. I took off my pants. I was somewhat hard by now. She helped me put it in. I pumped for a while. I wondered what she was thinking. The more I wondered, the softer it got. I came quickly. She seemed distracted. We said very little.

She got dressed and left. I felt bad.

Part 2. Write the same scene totally in metaphor. Allow it to sound utterly melodramatic, even like something out of a romance novel, if you want.

Example: My first time was decidedly awful—a disaster on a grand scale. I, a virgin college freshman, newly weaned from the teats of the repressed Jesuits at my all-male, suit-coat-and-tie dress code high school. She, an experienced, worldly JAP from Westchester. We, two ships on the choppy waters of sexual fulfillment. Or rather, me, a faulty canoe behind a well-outfitted cruise liner. My paddle was broken, needless to say. And when I finally fixed it, it was too late—she was already rolling her eyes in disappointment and disbelief at an all-too-brief fumbling, at my premature display of my rolling waves and ocean foam. Stranded, I watched in horror as my self esteem drowned in a huge sea of incompetence and sank like a heavy cold stone.

Review: With which exercise were you more comfortable and free with your writing? Which was more serious, more comic, more truthful, more interesting? How did changing the vocabulary affect your feeling about the episode? Do you remember it any differently now?

———————

The power of the written word stimulates the flow of emotions and readily opens the door to the subconscious. As you write, you will see how the resulting insight informs your conscious mind of the beliefs that are driving your life.

The River to the Subconscious

My "Freudian slips" turn out to be the golden
nuggets of my true feelings, which usually are covered over by my "appropriate" feelings.

—LORRAINE HOCHSTUHL, writing student

WRITING, AS THIS process prescribes, provides a direct
means of access to the imagination and the subconscious. The
stream-of-consciousness technique, when used as a tool for self-
exploration, allows us to forego the expectations of ourselves we typically have when talking or interacting. It can also reveal more than
most other forms of communication.

Because our subconscious mind is far more knowledgeable about
our thoughts and feelings than our conscious mind, slips of the
tongue or hand are valuable signals. They indicate that we are
touching upon sensitive or heretofore dangerous areas. Remember,
the hand speaks truer than the mind. Slips of the tongue or pen call
out for us to write directly about their subject.

Consider the words written by a student still groping with psychological damage caused by her father and first husband: "I'm
accused of always giving too much—whether it's time, money,
home, bed, food. Somebody, please tell *men* [instead of "me"],
what's too much? Another student, anxious about her income taxes,
referred to "CPR" rather than "CPA." A student whose deprecating
accounts of her neuroses would rival the comedy of Woody Allen
wrote that her writing was not fit for "humorous consumption." In
anticipation of a haircut, she wrote about committing "hairy kari."
Another student, in recording his sexual exploits, wrote about being
"immoralized" in place of "immortalized." Once, when I was experiencing a sensation of heat under my scalp, I found myself writing
about "steam of consciousness," an image that led me directly into
the "stream."

The consciousness that results from this writing process allows us to reclaim the authorship of our own lives. It gives us a medium in which to fearlessly plead for whatever we need to face our demons. It provides a sanctuary for dancing safely with the devil.

An Opportunity to Annihilate

Assignment: **Part 1.** Make a list of *people* who annoy you or make you angry. Do not hold back. Even a small annoyance qualifies. You do not have to know these people personally. They could be TV newscasters, your doctor's receptionist, or world leaders. Include members of your family, people you work with, neighbors, even teachers you had in grade school. As long as there is something—anything—about them that irritates or unsettled you, put them on the list.

Part 2. List *things* that annoy you or make you angry, for example, barking dogs, car alarms, long lines at the ATM machine, late mail delivery, shoddy craftsmanship, and so on.

Part 3. Create a scene in which you obliterate everything on both lists. Tear them up, burn them down, blow them away.

Review: Were you surprised by the number of items? Were they greater or fewer than you would have anticipated? How did you feel about your acts of destruction—were you gleeful, reluctant, impatient? Do you have any greater awareness of how much of your life is taken up with the negativity of anger and/or annoyance?

Writing Is Our Sanctuary

I return each night to my demon of the moment to
try and cajole him again with my coins. I hold him
gently in my left hand, as if I were a hostage assuag-
ing the anger of her captive. With my right hand,
I feverishly throw coins down his throat,
praying for a reprieve.

—ARLENE HUYSMAN, PH.D., writing student

A SANCTUARY IS a place for worship and cultivation of spirit.
It is a place of safety and refuge. At times this means a place of
order and tranquillity, a retreat away from disharmony. At other
times it means a place to indulge in creativity, to seek meaning in
life, to do the work of transformation, which often calls for descent
into pain and chaos. For the work of transformation, a sanctuary
provides a hallowed setting for embracing lurking shadows on hallowed ground. Writing provides just such a sanctuary.

Uncensored writing, both daily pages and the exercises in this
book, creates a safe place to vent, act out, fantasize, take revenge,
grieve, destroy, and plead. These daily pages are your uncondition-
ally accepting confessor and private oracle all in one.

Safety and reassurance are critical when stepping from the world
of one belief system into another. Our old stories have provided us
only with illusions of safety. Writing provides a safe place to apply
the power of these illusions to a story unbound by the familiar
restraints or parameters of the old ones. The process allows us to
forego the expectations we typically have when we are talking or
interacting. The more we practice, the keener our instincts grow
and the safer we feel about our own choices. We experience progressive emotional and physical release. With the resulting shifts in
our tastes, interests, and perspectives, "blocks" disappear and door
after door to creativity opens.

CHAPTER TWO

Write Three Pages and Call Me in the Morning!

*T*his writing offers a new way of seeing, often a way

of seeing at all. Sometimes it is an inky path through

a mental labyrinth, sometimes a silly poem,

sometimes an outpouring of thoughts I didn't

know were there.

—MARIAN SNEIDER, L.C.S.W., writing student

REGARDLESS OF WHETHER you are using this writing process as a diagnostic tool, healing procedure, or creative outlet, the results depend on regular practice, just as they do with any treatment or artistic discipline. The prescribed approach is as follows:

1. Write daily for at least five minutes or until you fill three full pages.

2. Disregard logic.

3. Suspend judgment toward anything you think or feel during the time you are writing.

4. Exaggerate everything!

5. Read it aloud to someone else.

Write Daily for at Least Five Minutes or Until You Fill Three Full Pages

This writing is a continual spilling of the beans.

—MONIKA BURG, writing student

I'd always thought I was kind of short on raw material for fiction. Now I realize that the simple truth is the best raw material there is.

—RICHARD SEVIGNY, writing student

THE PURPOSE OF the daily, free-form writing is to safely open the door to the great jumble of activity inside our minds. Careening from one topic to another can generate as much insight—and catharsis—as extended focus on a single thought. As a matter of fact, when we digress and the conscious mind relaxes, our defenses against taboo subjects relent, allowing the subconscious voice to make itself heard.

In the following writing example, a young college student veered from one subject to another, all along informing herself about her conflicted feelings concerning both her mother and freedom.

Mom never runs out of quarters. She is the person who has enough quarters in her ash tray to pay for an entire parking lot of

cars for the afternoon. Rarely does she ever end up in the
Receipts-Change line at the toll booth.

I used to love change. I thought that a pocket full of change
meant that you were rich. I loved the heaviness of my pocket
weighing down by my thigh, my fingers cupping the pennies
and nickels to make it a little lighter. Adults always seemed to
give away their change, like you were a wishing well or a foun-
tain where they could make their wishes come true. Yes. Maybe
they gave us their change in exchange for a silent promise that
we would follow through with their wishes. Be a good girl. Look
both ways before crossing the road. Say please and thank you.
Don't steal or chew with your mouth open. Find a nice a Jewish
boy and make sure he is a doctor. Don't be rude to your parents.

Rules. They are always there in front of you, surrounding you.
Somehow you manage to talk your way out of one of those "I forgot" situations, and then there they are again. I forgot to take out
the garbage. I forgot that I had an appointment. I forgot to call
you back. I'm sorry. But then there is that speed limit or that eti-
quette that you must deal with immediately after hanging up the
phone or apologizing to Mom. *Funny how Mom always enters
into these streams-of-consciousness,* like she is some scrambled
word I am always trying to unscramble or maybe trying to spell
correctly or maybe just trying to spell.

Sometimes it feels like a challenge to figure out what parts of
me, what letters, I have of her, all mixed up and undefinable. It
is nice not to be able to find her in some *Webster's* dictionary,
phonetically pronounced and having a two-part definition. She is
not a noun or a verb or an adjective. She is all.

All my life she has been with me. How can she not be in me
everywhere? In the way I fold my underwear, the way I brush my
hair, the way I organize, the people I am friends with, the hands
and the heart. Everywhere, like varicose veins on an elderly
woman. But beautiful. She is a characteristic of me and not one

of those wrinkles in the face of middle-aged woman. No, I don't want to get rid of her. At times I may want to cover her up so that people see me and not her in me. But most of the time I expose her, let her accentuate my beauty.

Sexy is not always swimsuit material. Sexy is the way Dave smiles in the morning with his breath of sleep fogging my face, the kind of fog that remains after a night of rain. Sexy is a little girl's curls falling across the straps of her yellow bathing suit. Sexy is the way cursive looks on parchment paper. The way the *y*'s and the *t*'s look. And the capitals, they look powerful and confident beside the smaller letters.

Vowels. I wanted to be a vowel when I was younger. There always seemed to be too many consonants, but somehow being a vowel meant that you could go in between the consonants and make them mean something. That meant that you were something, something important and needed.

I feel full of words and memories and pictures. I think I am going to start carrying around a tape recorder so that I can let them out to play. Nothing should ever stay inside if it wants to be free.

The threads of continuity among the subjects in this student's writing were as informative as the subjects themselves. Likewise, you can review much about your feelings and ideas by allowing yourself to veer and plunge from one topic to another.

Disregard Logic

It is a matter of getting out of the way of the flow,
instead of trying to direct it or—as I have tried to do
most of my life—shut it off. It means not censoring;
it means taking what I have been used to thinking of
as the dregs, the waste products of my mind, and

using them, not just as fertilizer, but as the raw
material of my creation.

—HORTENSE LEON, writing student

LOGIC DISTRACTS US from entering the subconscious where
ideas are freely synthesized. Judgment, censorship, or criticism of
any degree freezes our emotions and our creativity—along with the
healthy and therapeutic flow of physical energy. Judgment halts the
action in our personal story and deadens our awareness of the clues
to our condition—the metaphors all around us.

The habit of critical thinking has been especially reinforced in
our present scientific age, which reveres quantifiable data. Science
is based on the objective weighing of fact and detail, a mode of
"seeing without imagination." From the time we begin formal
learning, we are trained to measure, compare, and analyze. As a
professional design writer and art critic myself, I have made a
career of critical thinking. I know all too well its tenacity and
strength of resistance to the potential promiscuities of the explorative mind. "After all," whispers the critical mind, "just imagine
the mischief an undisciplined, unfocused, unexpurgated imagination might get into!" It could annihilate whole political parties or
nationalities. It could commit pagan acts and court eternal damnation. It could eat forbidden foods. It could do everything you've
ever restrained yourself from doing. It could let you see the hedo-
nist and anarchist—or puritan or fascist—that lurks inside you.
Here is an example:

This is insane. What am I doing . . . again? Another utterly
unavailable man. He's so intense. Self-contained. And hugely
resistant to me, to me in the way I want to be attended—for my
charm and sex appeal. Dragnet. As if I could drag a net around
him and haul him in and scream—me, me, ME! Pay attention to

me! But who the hell wants to haul? I just want to recline, swallow the peeled grapes, and crook my finger.

But nooooo. Once more, I go and draw a bead on a man on a mission. In fact, a real, true-to-life-god-damned missionary. You go, girl. Seduce a fucking priest. This makes no sense! None, and yet . . . why not? Ana says I'll burn in hell. Ok, how bad can hell be? Well, I could seduce him and he'd turn out to be the most attentive and passionate lover imaginable. Devoted. Devout. Gives up his mission for me. Gives up everything for me. Becomes my slave. Won't leave me for a second. Must serve me. Must adore me. Must whorship . . . I mean worship . . . at my feet and paint my toe nails. I wrote "whorship" instead of worship. Hmmmmmm. Is that what I think this would make me? An adored whole? I meant to write "whore" and wrote "whole." Hole, Courtney Love's band's name. Brilliant. A hole in hell. A hole in hell with a priest who devours me. Where would it end? If it's really hell, it would *never* end. Eternal burning . . . passion. Eternally being devoured. Eternal damnation for *wanting* attention. Both of us burned to ashes. And all the children of the world who were his original mission damned to lives of deprivation and hideous suffering . . . all because I couldn't keep away from a man with a mission.

Suspend Judgment Toward Anything You Think or Feel During the Time You Are Writing

A colleague I once consulted about writing dialogue advised me, "Just write down all those imaginary conversations you have with people in your head." My response was, "What conversations? I don't have imaginary conversations with people."

> Now I see that I do have these conversations
> all the time. I just keep censoring them. Like
> dreams, they don't go away just because they
> aren't acknowledged.

—HORTENSE LEON, writing student

BABIES FILTER NOTHING, censor nothing, and care nothing about the meaning of their actions. They feel what they feel—and respond accordingly, unconcerned about the acquired perceptions that later form their psyches. Our subconscious minds remain just as sensitive as a baby's, recording every thought and every feeling.

The simple observation of our judgments releases them. But we cannot observe what we do not allow. This writing process enables us to return to that infantile state of pure responsiveness and observe our thoughts and actions uncritically. Consciousness, another word for awareness, grows only as we allow ourselves to hear and see *all* our thoughts *without judgment*.

Consider the words of one student whom I asked to write about no longer having to demonstrate her need to make herself miserable.

I no longer have to demonstrate my need to make myself miserable. That feels like a lie. I think I would like it to be true, but I am not sure. Maybe I should run for public office where every wart is up for public display. Where the fear is really shame. Shame of being human, imperfect, unaccepting of my narcissism, not wanting it to show.

I forever believed I would shame my mother, let her down if I were not perfect in her eyes. Surely if I got sick and died it would kill her. She died this past February, two weeks before her ninety-eighth birthday. My sadness was mixed with relief: I can't shame her anymore.

I don't need to stay stuck in this stuff. Yes, maybe I'll run for office. Look, Bill Clinton's medical records indicate that he is taking Maalox and an acne medication. So he has gas pains and acne and the whole world knows it. Have we shame here? No. In fact, the Maalox stock will go up. Indigestion will become *de rigeur.*

Exaggerate Everything and Embrace the Ridiculous!

OUR SUBCONSCIOUS MINDS are exaggerating everything anyway, so we might as well get it all out on paper. To the subconscious, off-balance is full tilt. Out of alignment is total distortion. Any hollowness means no wholeness. While we may be telling ourselves that we are feeling only small annoyance, our subconscious minds are interpreting our feelings as all-out assault. A minor hurt is as bad as a major attack. So project your subconscious feelings into wide-screen, surround-sound Technicolor and see them in all their melodramatic glory. Embellish the drama. Embroider the truth. Massacre, smash, throb, soar, pummel, demand, desecrate. Commit heresy, treachery, infanticide. Create a spectacular fiction out of the mundanity in your life. You may be surprised at what you see on the page, but it can liberate and enlighten you.

The effect of conscious exaggeration is manyfold: The cartoonish quality it gives our scenarios releases us from our fixed identification with them; ridiculous exaggeration diminishes the power lurking in unexpressed issues; inflating the issue increases our awareness of how much space, time, energy, and emotion it occupies in our lives.

If I don't hit a grand slam with my career soon, I'll die. I'll just curl up and bury myself under home plate, or under my house, like the place under the house where the dogs used to sleep.

That's where I'll live out my life, in the dirt with the dogs. No! No! No! Much as I love the animals and the safe darkness of hiding out, hiding out at home, hiding out at home under the house, I *still* want to hit one out of the park.

I climb out of the dugout, walk onto the playing field one more time, step up to the plate and this time . . . wham! A grand slam! Every one of my projects hits the charts. The phone rings off the hook. Money floods my bank account. Bill Gates gets worried that I'll out-distance him, that I, instead of he, will be the richest man in history. And then what? Then I have to worry about how history records my efforts. Fuck it! Like hell, I'm going to worry. The whole idea was to knock my ambitions right out of the ball park, round the bases, and collect the rewards for decades of labor and sustained faith—and be fucking proud of myself. Is this what it takes? Do I believe I have to surpass Bill Gates to be worthy of my own admiration?

Read It Aloud to Someone Else

Isolation fosters paralysis. Shared expression
fosters trust.

—ALINA PANTERA, teacher

READING YOUR WRITING aloud to someone else is a potent catalyst. This action can be frightening, even terrifying. After all, simply allowing your thoughts out of our head and into your hand is intimidating enough. Equally scary, is letting the feelings out of your hand and onto the page, and from the page to your eyes. Then, scariest of all, into your conscious mind! You may think, "How could I possibly share my ugliest beliefs with anyone else when I can barely stand to hear them myself?" However, the more willing you are to lose your reputation with yourself, the faster and deeper your awareness grows.

In *Women Who Run with the Wolves,* Clarissa Pinkola Estes explains how the "spoken story touches the auditory nerve, which runs across the floor of the skull into the brainstem just below the pons. There, auditory impulses are relayed upward to consciousness or else, it is said, to the soul . . . depending on the attitude with which one listens."

She tells how ancient storytellers considered the auditory nerve to be divided into three or more pathways deep inside the brain. They surmised, therefore, that the ear was meant to hear at three different levels. "One pathway was said to hear the mundane conversations of the world. A second pathway apprehended learning and art. And the third existed so the soul itself might hear guidance and gain knowledge while here on earth."

By reading aloud to a listener you further neutralize your attachment to your beliefs. You cultivate feelings of security about expressing yourself to others or exposing your thoughts and feelings publicly. Of course, you never have to read aloud if a subject is too difficult or if you are not yet ready to express it aloud. However, just as with the writing, it is important to acknowledge your fear or resistance. It's also important to test your limits and sometimes take a deep breath and plunge.

In my class we not only read aloud, but I also assign students a different writing partner weekly to whom they read their daily pages aloud over the phone each day. One partner reads while the other listens silently, without interruption; then they switch. The listening partner is not to comment, sympathize, or advise. If the two partners wish to share conversation after they have read to one another, that is their choice. I do not encourage it. The point of this work is not to further enroll yourself or others in each other's old stories.

The act of reading your writing aloud to another person stimulates responses distinct from those you have when writing. One student described it this way: "I read slowly, even when reading silently to myself. I need to hear the words in order to fully comprehend. To give them their full due . . . respect. I have bothered to write my story—now I will listen and hear it."

Some students, on the other hand, who initially feel deeply apprehensive about reading aloud, eventually come to realize the source of their discomfort. "I will never read to my partners ever!" wrote one after only a few days of writing and reading. "I will *never again* take the time to share my writing or expose my feelings. Shit, I've done enough sharing. Now I want attention, *all* the attention. And I don't want to have to get on the phone to find it! I mean nobody wants to hear what I have to say, anyway. No, actually, it's just *me* who doesn't want to hear what I have to say. It's only me who's bored with the still, small voice and is looking for some razzmatazz."

Here is another student's reaction to the reticence of her reading partners:

> When I ask you to read over the telephone, I feel your fingers cringe, holding the pen. Why are you so vulnerable? Why are you so afraid of sharing? Why is it so hard (for you) to share the written word? Why is the spoken word easier? When reading the written word, it's solid, it's permanent, it's there. You are afraid to chip away at your mind, to look for that bit of shining quartz that you can use, polish, and wear proudly. Are you afraid you may not find it? That there may be no gold?

Fear of having nothing valuable to write or read may well be the most common fear of all. I can only assure you that transformation is the inherent result of daily writing and reading aloud.

If a reading becomes very emotional, perhaps prompting tears or anger, partners have several choices. The reader can pause, continue, or stop altogether. The listener must not get involved but instead remain quietly present, allowing the reader to do what feels best. By allowing the reader time, the listener also gains the opportunity to silently acknowledge her own feelings about the content of the writing.

Wait quietly—for the partner's answer and for your own.

I suggest to those who are not in some kind of writing class or group that they identify an appropriate friend or family member who is willing to listen silently and confidentially. Explain how the process works, and remind this person that you are not seeking advice or response.

Listen for your own "energy spots," sensitive or unexpected places where your deeper issues lie. These are your next assignments, the subjects calling for your attention, asking for you to write about them.

If your reading partner wishes to respond to your writing, ask her to write it out in the technique we are using for this process and then to read her writing to you. What she is hearing and responding to is likely just as much about herself as it is about you. Her writing will help to make this clearer and will also diffuse whatever emotion may be attached to her response.

Allow the Process to Unfold Like a Story

THERE ARE NO predetermined endings with this transformational work. Like baseball and romance, the process takes as long as it takes to reach its conclusion. It unfolds chapter by chapter, without regard for expectation.

When I wrote about "turning to stone," I expected to feel anguish. Deep anguish. But the truth is . . . I love stone. Terra cotta. Terra firma. Keystone. Coral rock. Malachite. Lapis lazuli. Precious, semi-precious, permeable, concrete, pourous, earthen. I love stone. Terra cotta. Terra firma. Terra dolorosa.

The stations of the cross. Via dolorosa. A path of stones, stones permeated with blood and tears. Worn. Worn smooth. Worn sharp. Veil of tears. Shroud of cries. And I thought "turning to stone" meant cold numbness.

You may feel like tasting and digesting small portions of your exploration process at one time and devoting yourself to deep immersion at others. What is important is to be conscious of your choices—and to tell yourself the truth (e.g., "I only have the stamina right now to face my feelings in small bits" or "I want immediate clarity, and I'm willing to delve until I get it"). You must respect the pace at which your stories unfold while sustaining attention to them.

CHAPTER THREE

The Gifts of This Writing

*I*knew that in order to survive I had to return to my skewed foundation and see it straight. . . . I wrote with the eyes of the damaged little boy who had been pursued, seduced, loved, chastised, and abandoned. And only after I had written with those eyes could I begin to see with my own adult eyes. Then the terror moved out of my head. Then out of my body. For the first time I felt I could truly trust myself.

—BARRY ZAID, writing student

Symbolic sight is a way of seeing and understanding yourself, other people, and life events in terms of universal archetypal patterns. Symbolic sight lets you see into your spirit and your limitless potential for healing and wholeness.

—CAROLINE MYSS, PH.D., *Anatomy of the Spirit*

Transformation occurs in context,
rather than in content.

—ALINA PANTERA, teacher

Heightened Intuition and Clarity

I DEFINE INTUITION as sensory intelligence. Because our present culture is far more focused on cerebral intelligence, we tend to insufficiently honor the knowing that comes to us through taste, touch, sound, scent, and imagery. Yet these provide worlds of information and guidance that cerebral response alone does not even address.

The more we honor our senses, the more clearly we perceive. With greater trust in our perceptions, we gain faith in our desires. This frees us to venture into aspects of our imaginations we would previously have judged unsuitable or unworthy. Our internal and external worlds expand. Knowing better our own strengths, we no longer fear misjudgment.

As we transfer our thoughts from the mind to the page, we simultaneously shift energy into our senses. The simple recording of our feelings and observations provides a distance between them and our habitual judgments. This allows our sensory abilities to grow. Where criticism once framed the sound, color, taste, and touch of an experience, a whole new spectrum of sensation can flood—or trickle—in.

Our writing provides a context in which we can safely "feel the fear and do it anyway." Change does not occur in a static environment or as a result of varying a theme. Change comes about when, in challenging our behaviors and perceptions, we recognize another way of being. Through our writing we can try out ideas under totally fictional circumstances and learn of our aptitudes and inclinations, our resistances and challenges.

A Walk in the Dark

Assignment: You are undergoing an initiation in which you must walk blindfolded. It is up to you to choose the location, the person who can accompany you, and whatever you will bring along with you. Do you choose a beach, woods, suburban street, city sidewalk? Who will your partner be? Do you do this in bare feet, shoes, boots, or other protective footwear? What do you bring along with you, if anything?

Example: I'm walking down St. Pete beach at night, with E., hand in hand. "Close your eyes," he says. I am thrilled. An adventure. An adventure and I am in his hands. We are walking in the dark. The stars are out and the waves barely kissing the shore, but I see none of it except the comforting blackness behind my eyelids—and it is such a relief. An exhilarating relief. I could do this forever. Walk barefoot on the hard-packed sand into night and day and endless horizon, my hand in his, without seeing anything but this comforting blanket of blackness.

This is the first time my eyes have felt rested in months—they've been aching and fatigued for so long that I can't remember what it was ever like to rest them. Searching for the answers. I've worn my eyes out searching for answers, for clues. Now I am being led. Into darkness. On hard-packed sand in bare feet. And I love it.

Review: What did this assignment tell you about your sense of trust in another person and in your own senses? What did it tell you about the environments in which you feel safest, and your need (or lack of need) for planning and equipment?

Example: At the time I loved E. Would nearly have put my life in his hands. But instinct told me, be circumspect. How circumspect can you be in the dark? I do love the dark, and with him, apparently, I loved being kept in the dark. It was the light of truth that hurt.

I'd read in the dark if I could. Light, like summer glare, summer sun, is harsh. Too much. Too much input. Too much information. I don't want to see too much. I want to rest my eyes and my body and my sense of touch all in the comfort of darkness. Like being barefoot. I love touching the earth. Simple, naked foot-to-earth, night air and darkness.

And yet my life is about vision, about perception. I notice now that as my eyes grow weaker with age, my sense of touch and tactile order seem to be taking over where the weakness leaves off. I sculpt more with my hands than with my eyes. Well, maybe not more, but at least as much these days. Goodbye tiny gouache paintings with gold-leafed details and little tiny crocheted fine wire pieces. Hello monumental sculpture.

Often, what we want most also frightens us most. We doubt that we deserve it, or we fear the changes it will bring. At other times we convince ourselves—because of cultural or family conditioning—that we want something, which, in fact, we don't want at all. Our blurred vision keeps us groping along the same familiar, but unsatisfying, path. Until we see clearly what we want, we remain flailing about in the self-created fog that sustains our illusion of safety.

When we are willing to see clearly, we perceive what we want. By writing daily, we can cut through the fog and discover a fully dimensional view of our hearts' desires. This is how one student describes the experience of learning to trust her desire to leave her high-paying corporate job for a sabbatical of self-exploration:

I'd become so tired of the rat maze that I decided to go away and build a new life. I'd assumed the new life would be as exciting as the old life, but the excitement didn't happen. I panicked when I realized my assumption that I could return to my old life was false. I knew that if I tried to be the person I once was, I'd simply die—even though I'd been perfectly happy being that person for the first 40 years of my life. And now what?

I figured that eventually I'd realize that the past wasn't entirely bad and that once I was relaxed, I could "go back." Then I remembered that this was exactly the attitude that had kept me unhappily locked tight for years. I began to think I was on a long, slippery slope downhill, and I didn't know what was at the bottom.

Then, lo and behold, I started to enjoy the slide—feeling the wind in my face and the sense of freedom. I didn't even care if I ever reached bottom. I had faith there'd be a swimming pool there to catch me.

Now I'm beginning to want to steer myself into the "right" pool. I'm beginning to care about the slide. I'm beginning to search for an opportunity to land. At first "playing" was just a way to forget my problems. Now it's become a way to realize I have fewer problems than I thought. Sometimes it's difficult to tell the difference between the poison and the antidote, so I have to risk being poisoned. Anything but going back!

I want to connect the dots, but I'm still not sure which dots to connect and which to leave out. As if I've hit the water and am slowly surfacing. Part of me can't help floating up to whatever place gravity pulls me. The other part is beginning to swim under water to a warm spot in the pool. Although I don't know exactly where I'm going, I can't regret the slide, even though most people would say it was a destructive, wasteful amusement.

I'm beginning to anticipate adult swimming, even though I miss my little friends. The most amazing thing is that I want to swim again, after thinking I might just float for the rest of my life.

Your Heart's Desire

Assignment: You have been offered the job of your dreams, or the love of your life, or a considerable fortune, whichever you desire most. Accepting this, however, means moving to the other side of the world and completely uprooting yourself from your present life. How would this affect those closest to you, especially those dependent on you? Write out what it would be like to accept the job, lover, or fortune and the results.

Example: If I moved to Europe, Mom would be most affected because I'd have to leave all my stuff at her house. Of course she can never say no, and then she's also the Keeper of Clutter and could not bear to ever see another person's clutter wasted. So my stuff would sit in her house, taking over the antiques room in mountains of junk so high that no one could get to the desk. She'd hop around all the boxes, and with the weight of my stuff added to the weight of her stuff, one of the mountains is sure to tip over and fall down on her, like a ball and chain. She is buried in the avalanche, never to emerge from all that stuff. Grandma had to die to get away. (Did she know on a spiritual level?) That must be why it took her only a month to die. Could you ever imagine taking that house and Mom simultaneously!

Review: How much anxiety did you feel as you started the assignment? Did it increase or diminish as you were writing?

Example: I suddenly realized how much I've been putting this thought out of my head. The thought of accepting her offer, of letting her give too much . . . again. I'd been ignoring the effect it would have on her; I'd been thinking only about all the things I'd have to be without.

Do I feel different after writing? Yes! Knowing on a conscious level that I'm contributing to my mother's bondage. I cannot bear to do that. I need to refocus myself.

Assignment: Write out the opposite scene—one in which you give up the job, lover, or fortune in order to stay put exactly where you are for the rest or your life.

Example: My headaches become more frequent. My face is puffy. I have a chronic cold and cough. I feel like crying. I keep dreaming that I'm being flushed down the toilet like a meager piece of dirty something.

   And then the regret. Why didn't I take the chance! What's the big deal—I've taken chances before. I feel like I'm in my own prison of confusion, and black weights are holding me back. I'm chained to the past, to my mother, to the deaf and dumb.

Review: Did you feel relief or disappointment? What surprised you most, if anything, about both scenarios?

Example: The relief. The horror. Going. NOT going! I didn't think staying, I didn't think giving up my dreams would make me THAT sick. But it would. It would be unendurable.

This student's writing absolutely clarified the correctness of her decision to move and made her aware of the responsibilities connected with it. The writing brought into view not only the focus of her questioning but the peripheral issues as well.

Growing Fearlessness

Openly revealing our feelings establishes credibility.
We are what we feel.

—GERRY SPENCE, *How to Argue and Win Every Time*

ONCE WE RECOGNIZE what we truly want, we must acknowledge any fears that hinder or delay its manifestation. Strange as it sounds, fulfillment can be highly intimidating. Much as we might proclaim a hatred for scarcity—of money, relationships, sex, or even health—we must still recognize how or where that poverty serves us. For example, if we declare that we want wealth, we must see what we will be relinquishing to have it. Relinquish? What could there possibly be to give up when we already have too little, we might ask. A terrific excuse, for one thing. A justification for saying no, a reason for not giving time, funds, or attention. A great way out and a great way of holding on to a needy identity. An effective way of getting sympathy or staying attached to those to whom we are indebted, sometimes with resentment or vengeance.

This writing process gives us the means to try out the scenario of fulfillment. The more developed our mechanisms for coping with scarcity, the harder it can be to disassemble them. In our writing we can preview what would happen when we get what we truly want.

Great Regret

Assignment: Complete a sentence that begins "If I were to risk . . . " and keep writing, totally exaggerating your fears and their consequences.

Example: If I were to risk moving back to New York, I would be overwhelmed with regret about my present life. And, in fact, I have started to feel regretful lately. I wonder if regret has the power to take us anywhere, to make us do anything. Would my regrets move me to take this risk? And why would moving back to New York be such a risk anyway?

Is it because I don't want to work? Then I'm damn right to stay here. New York is not a place for the lazy. It is a city of slaves. I'd have to wait tables at B's restaurant. I should be grateful; after all I still have the looks, if not the capacity to do the job. I can fool people for a day or two.

Then, of course, I couldn't afford to live in Manhattan, so I'd be out in Brooklyn, taking the subway in on Saturday nights to get drunk. I don't know why I always drink in New York.

Review: Did you include every possible consequence? If not, write about how much you'd rather *not* write about the one(s) you excluded.

Example: New York ten years down the line. All the money I make, I drink. I swallow it. I smell it, and I sweat it. I vomit it. I can't think of anything but sex. I'm lonely, broke, broken in this modern Middle Age town. My apartment has roaches and a mouse that's been dead forever. I have no life, no friends. I'm a nobody. With Caller ID, you can't even get a soul on the phone.

My Belgian friends used to say, "Enjoy the risk! It's not enough to take the risk. You've got to enjoy it!" Well, it's never happened that way for me . . . and it never will! I couldn't enjoy the New York risk. The risk would be ME—in my flesh, every day. I would find out that the phone never rings when you're alone. That you pass out in your chair whether you have an alcohol or a solitude hangover. I would know that the phone won't ring when you're out of work. It simply won't! Don't buy a Caller ID if you lose your job—you don't need one!

Review: How likely are these consequences? What did you realize from this writing? Do you find it easier to write about the past, the present, or the future?

Example: Likely or not, I realized that I am my own risk. Doing nothing more with my life than trying to become a writer, that's a bet in itself, isn't it? Maybe there's no other risk for me than this one. Maybe I don't move to New York because I know this. And maybe that's a risk too.

Example: Regardless of how likely any consequences are, I am learning to grow. Yes, I am growing every minute, even when the storm is the heaviest. . . . I am learning to survive. How I need to go inside myself, to learn who I am.

The next two weeks will not be filled with easy tasks. My plate is full, too full. But what is strange is that I see the tasks as events on the calendar . . . nothing more.

I must learn to live in the present. I worry about the future. I bask in its possibilities. Therefore, the hell with the next two weeks! Fuck tomorrow! Who am I right now? How do I feel right now?

Am I lonely this minute? Am I torn with depression right now? NO . . . absolutely not. I am present . . . right here now.

Manifestation requires *wholeness*—of our physical, emotional, mental, and spiritual being. Regret and doubt puncture wholeness, sabotage holiness. We must trust our own power in order to sustain its manifestations.

Increased Power

Liberation means letting go all that stands in the way
of your new creation.

—ALINA PANTERA, teacher

THE MEASURE OF power we possess relies on the measure of power we are *willing* to possess. Our power is determined by how much of our old stories we are willing to relinquish in favor of our new creation. We must ask ourselves if we are willing to surrender

THE GIFTS OF THIS WRITING 55

those stories fed to us throughout our lives by that constellation of family, religion, and culture. Are we willing to revise them, discard them, even betray them if necessary? How much are we willing to let go of?

When you write about your willingness to let go of old, destructive stories, you discover exactly what stands in the way of your new creation. Your writing will also reveal how willing you are to let go of your "impediments." You will learn whether, in fact, you are at all willing to do what is necessary, to change to whatever degree, and in whatever form.

Frankly, many people are unwilling to take these risks, even to save a relationship, a career, or their own lives. Sadly, they prefer to stay mired in their suffering rather than to change their beliefs about themselves and others. They would rather be "right" than healthy, prosperous, safe, or fulfilled. Even if given a precise map to their truest desire, they would forego it rather than venture into "unworthy" territory. Doing this work demonstrates the healing power of nonjudgmental disclosure. Only when we are willing to see ourselves and the world differently can this, or any other process, change our lives.

Truth or Not?

Assignment: Write a scene in which you say no to your mother, stand up to your brother, or decline an invitation from a family member or friend by fabricating a convenient and believable, but untrue, story. As the story evolves, exaggerate it until it is totally outrageous.

Example: How am I going to say no to my mother? She has sent me the money for the tickets. She's booked our tour of Morocco. How can I tell her that we can't make it? That *I* can't make it. That I can't tolerate even the thought of this trip.

I have to tell her that there was a sinkhole in my property. That my house was disappearing by the minute, that the earth had opened up like a big volcano hole and we were being consumed. The mice and the possum that live under the house are moving into the bedrooms. The cats are so freaked that they want to hide with the snake, of which they are terrified. At least the snake has a solid cage. The girls are crying constantly.

The engineers I've called cannot control it. They started filling in the hole with earth and sand to see if they could prevent the breaking down of the foundations. But no—wherever they filled, it just opened up more. I have my own private earthquake going on.

The TV stations are recording it. We're on the national news. No more privacy. We have to watch out for our house, and yet it's disappearing! Mother, how can we come now?

Review: How did you feel as you were writing this believable lie? Did your feelings change as the story grew exaggerated? Did you feel more detached? Safer or more vulnerable?

Example: I'm scared of envisioning tragedies of any kind and when I do, I usually cancel them out and replace them with wonderful satisfying images. So, at first, I was apprehensive about imagining that something could go wrong with our summer plans with Mother. Because I haven't seen her in two years, and this trip is a big deal in our healing from five years of silence. Yet the images gave me relief and strength. And made me laugh.

Assignment: Write the same scene, but this time tell only the truth. Describe the potential consequences of your honest response. Are you disinherited? Does your mother commit suicide? Will your brother never lend you money again? Will your friends never invite you over again?

Example: Hello, Mummy. I don't know how to say this. We can't make it. We're just too scared of you, of how argumentative you are. Of how you always have to be right. I remember when I was thirteen and we traveled through Spain and you put a cigarette out on the back of Popi's hand because he didn't agree with you.

The girls say you are too critical. That you never listen.

Oh, I know you've gone to this big expense.

Hello, Popi. I'm sorry to disappoint you. But we're not coming.

Hello. Hello.

They hung up.

Review: Where in your body were you most uncomfortable as you wrote this scene? What would your life be like without this feeling of obligation? How likely are the consequences you described? Are you willing to face them at this time? If no, do you believe there will ever be a time when you are?

Example: My neck. My head. My lower back. An assault.

If I didn't feel obliged to please my mother, to learn to love her, I probably would feel freer to love D. without judging him so harshly for speaking English with the "wrong" accent. I wouldn't be so demanding and critical with myself.

Consequences? Another five years of silence? An eternity of silence? A gaping wound never, ever healed? Could I face this? I just don't know.

———————

By using your writing to exercise truth telling, you strengthen your ability to rely on truth. With this strength comes faith.

Broadened Patience

THE CIRCUMSPECTION THAT results from this writing increases our ability to await the manifestation of our dreams and desires. Articulation enhances anticipation with concrete imagery. It allows us to build steadily rather than acting impulsively to get what we think we want. It provides rehearsal time: time to determine the most comfortable settings, flattering costumes, and supportive casts, time to fire inadequate technicians, to discard whatever hinders the action in the play of our lives, and to safely respond to that release.

By supplying insight, the writing also broadens our patience with ourselves. By feeding the imagination, it gives us a wealth of options and fresh ideas. With this stimulation and creativity, impatience dissolves.

Nothing Changes

Assignment: It is five years from now and nothing, not one thing, has changed in your life. What does your life look like, sound like, smell like, and feel like?

Example: My God, No!!! A life of settling and drudgery. Ed and I in that one bedroom apartment—two big fish swimming around in a tiny bowl, unable to grow. If only we had an ocean, we would grow magnificently. But no, we're stuck here, swimming circles around each other, trying to get away.

I go into the next room (there are only two). But I still hear the droning of his TV through the wall. We switch rooms, but I know he's just on the other side, and I'm tied down, stuck. And Peter, my glorious Viking whom I enjoyed for only one glorious night, is fading from my mind. Just another story for my autobiography. Ed is just on the side of the wall, and I don't want to go to bed ever again, for he's there.

Assignment: Reverse the assignment. It is five years from now, and your greatest wishes have come true.

Example: I have accepted the love of my life and am moving far away. First Peter and I live together in California, and then we move to Sweden. At first I was scared, now I'm exuberant. Mom is the only one who is in any way disturbed about it. She said she wanted to take the motor home to come visit, and my only thought was, Thank God My Mother Cannot Drive a Motor home To Sweden!

Anxiety is all gone.

Review: How much more complete was your picture after you wrote than before? Which aspects of this picture give the most delight, and which ones cause you second thoughts?

Example: Of course the idea of being with Peter gives me complete delight. Before, when I thought about this, I was so horrified about moving to Sweden that my throat literally closed up, blocked the fifth chakra and I couldn't speak. Just like my students—I'll be struggling with Swedish just like they struggle with English. I see now that this was more what the fear was about than the distance. Every time I opened my mouth, I'd cough. It was my fear of being unable to communicate.

I am certain that by now this writing technique has become familiar and your thoughts more fluid. Different applications for the process have probably occurred to you. The blank page is less intimidating, and you may even look forward to picking up the pen.

You now have a tool—a solid, reliable, and completely trust-worthy tool that is always and entirely at your disposal. In the next chapter you will learn how to apply this tool specifically for transformation.

CHAPTER FOUR

Six Classic Principles of Transformation

*A*dmire the world . . . as you would admire an

opponent, without taking your eyes off him,

or walking away.

—ANNIE DILLARD, author

CONSCIOUS OBSERVATION PRODUCES change. This, in essence, is a law of quantum physics. This writing, as a form of observation, moves us from "trance formation" to transformation.

Regardless of whether the transformation we seek is from need to abundance, from disease to health, or from struggle to ease, it cannot be made in leaps and bounds. Safely, the process can be taken only one step at a time.

Leaps, in the physical world, require muscle and choreography. Unpracticed, they are dangerous to body and spirit and can leave us cripplingly unbalanced. Imbalance fosters doubt, doubt prompts fear, and fear leads to regression and paralysis. Only a step-by-step progression allows us the security we need for successful and sustained transformation.

The Six Classic Principles of Transformation provide a foundation upon which we can take incremental steps in the outer world while indulging leaps of the imagination. The more mindful we become of how these principles operate in our lives, the more quickly and accurately we will be able to identify underlying motivations for our feelings and actions.

The practice of recognizing these principles in our own minds and in others' actions intensifies our abilities to hear, observe, and intuit. Applying the principles trains us to hear more clearly our own thoughts and beliefs, to observe more keenly how the world mirrors these thoughts and beliefs, and to sense more acutely how and where the activity of the conscious and subconscious minds affects our physical bodies.

Practicing the Six Classic Principles of Transformation increases our awareness of exactly how we create, promote, and/or allow chronic situations to perpetuate in our lives. When we apply the principles to recollections of our history and observe how they operate in others, we can see exactly how thoughts and expressions affect our levels of power—some thoughts magnifying it, others insidiously or flagrantly leeching it from the cells of tissues where memory is stored.

"Wait a minute!" I hear many people in my classes cry. "You're telling me that *I'm* creating, promoting, allowing for the pain, turmoil, and struggle that plagues my life and disrupts my happiness?"

Yes, I am saying exactly that. "How could weak men who are terrified of commitment, demanding women who are impossible to satisfy, parasitic children who refuse to take responsibility for their own lives, corporate downsizing, unfair child support laws, headaches, backaches, allergies, PMS, heart trouble, cancer, addiction, or AIDS possibly serve me?" students demand in indignation.

The answer is simple—and a great rub to the ego. Chronic issues or patterns of circumstance serve to keep us enrolled in our stories.

They perpetuate the trances we have cast upon ourselves in our chosen roles as victim, survivor, rescuer, loyal supporter, traitor, savior, romantic, realist, good parent, black sheep. We break the spell by recognizing exactly what we have done in the past and continue to do in the present to create, promote, or allow our own pain.

The Six Classic Principles of Transformation

1. What you resist persists.

2. What you acknowledge increases.

3. What you withhold is withheld from you.

4. All perception is projection.

5. You get not what you want, but what you believe.

6. What you give out is what you want most.

What You Resist Persists

NEGATIVE THOUGHTS ACCUMULATE power and momentum in direct proportion to the measure of resistance applied to them. *Unconscious* denial of anger, jealousy, guilt, shame, grief, or despair only deepens a wound. Unconscious resistance to these feelings similarly generates negative energy, keeping the psyche connected to the pain. Surrender to feelings dissipates that energy and brings the psyche into a state of neutrality that fosters healing. Writing provides a safe medium for surrender and saves us from acting on negative feelings impulsively, insensitively, or inappropriately.

"It seems to me that shadows are of supreme importance in perspective," wrote Leonardo da Vinci. This is no less true in writing and healing than in great painting, for our shadows know *all* our fears, weaknesses, and doubts. It is, in fact, their very embodiment.

Conscious resistance or denial facilitates surrender. Without consciousness, there can be no substantial release. The bigger the conscious resistance the deeper the release and the broader the insight. Many healing and spiritual traditions express this concept of surrender as "making an ally of the enemy." We can learn from our shadows—the persona we have buried out of shame, guilt, or critical judgment. Our shadows show us how to adopt the tools of the opposition and ultimately embrace what we have long fought.

We can, through writing, stalk our shadows until they become our allies. Instead of reviling or running from our alter egos, we diminish them through the glare of the spotlight; we eliminate them by swallowing and digesting them; we steal their fear-producing capacity by embracing them.

To stalk the shadows, we must ask any and all questions about ourselves, about our family, and about life all around us. As we "sniff out" clues about the shadows' hold on us, we grow free to discover the deepest answers to our darkest questions. We grow strong enough to reclaim the power we once gave over to the shadows for its use against us.

With our writing, we first *assist* the resistance—the shadow—before surrendering to it. We do this by imagining an anxiety-causing scenario in far greater dimension. We let our imagination run to the farthest extremes, totally indulging in whatever emotion, drive, fear, desire, or condition plagues us.

There is an important difference between this mental play and common neurotic obsession: With this technique we are indulging thoughts out of conscious choice rather than out of unconscious habit. And consciousness expands our power. Furthermore, the exaggerated picture we write informs us rather than distracts us. It reveals how ludicrously unrealistic our fears are and/or how deeply they pervade our minds. Either way, the extreme description presents our fears in different perspective, enabling us to more readily surrender them.

A clinical psychologist whose practice was consuming her came to my class seeking to regain some sense of control over her life. I assigned her to first write about a typical day, making no effort in the writing to restrain its pace.

Speeding

I've just arrived, out of breath, from my last stop of the day, a day which has now moved into night. Now that I write about this, I realize I've been right about not wanting to stop and take time for myself. I did that for a brief time this morning and the stopping was so painful, so devastating, that I wanted not just to walk, but to run, better yet, to fly, away from the scene.

I wanted to get right back on the daily treadmill of my life and start running again. I jumped into my car, already one hour late for my first appointment. Behind the wheel, I was aware that I was speeding, going at least 70 mph. I scanned the road for a police car. Did I want to be stopped?

My stomach was growling. Was it hunger or aggravation? Another ulcer, perhaps? I arrived at last and rushed into the office, unable to even hear the apology being offered me by a colleague who had wronged me. I couldn't even wait for my associate to finish his sentence to the group he was working with, but was forced by my own inner turmoil to say, "Let's go— we're late!"

We rushed out. It was raining and I noticed that my associate seemed frightened that I would drive at my usual breakneck speed. Out of the first sane impulse of the day, I gave him the keys.

Through this writing, the student gained a view of the pace she had created for herself and was willing to surrender—to relin-

quish in her writing her resistance to slowing down and stopping.
I asked her to create a scene in which she was stuck in a chair,
unable to move out of it for hours or days at a time. Here is her
response:

Chair Bound

I arise only to greet and dismiss. I have much to say to these
people, but that is not allowed. I have been mandated only to listen.

Oh, the thousand and one stories, voices lamenting, crying
out for relief. They ring ceaselessly in my ears. And then there is
another thousand voices, speaking in tongues about sheer trivial-
ities.

Maybe I'll explode with all this knowledge and unexpressed
feeling. Maybe my ass will spread so out of proportion to my
head that someone will notice my crisis and save me.

Or maybe I'll finally open my mouth to speak and a never-
ending wail will float out into eternity. Maybe my unending wail
will help all the suffering people who have deposited their trou-
bles into me.

Wouldn't such feelings of captivity not make anyone want to
run—or fly—away! With this writing, the psychologist began to see
how her frantic pace served to keep her from the imagined torture of
being "chair bound." She realized that the source of her unease was
not her pace but rather her potential captivity. With the recognition
that the extremity of the feared scenario was of her own making, she
calmed both her conscious and subconscious minds and was then
able to temper her rapid-fire pace. Without this recognition, any
amelioration of the situation would have proved temporary.

Another student wrote:

It's true. The thing I've feared most for two years is about to happen. I've spent almost all my money refusing to return to my old life—but without finding a new alternative. What if in the end I'm forced to do what I've been avoiding all this time—get the same job with another company and lead a miserable life surrounded by "prison" inmates. All because I've waited too long to take care of myself. I've been so busy looking for the perfect answer, I've found no answer.

A student who complained about writer's block was "having a hard time connecting to myself, to the past, and to others." I suggested she dive into her ennui to see what it fulfilled for her.

Living Life to the Least

My father used to watch me write, standing at my back. He'd circle words in red and scream. Eventually I improved, and he became almost proud of me . . . until I played my last little card. "What do we want to be when we grow up?" he asked. I had my answer ready, and that answer still frightens me.

I want not to be anything or anyone. I want to avoid having an identity, a history, even a country or a set of furniture. I don't want to be attached to anything.

Freedom? Is that what they call freedom? I doubt it. Freedom is action. I don't want to "do." I want to be undone. I want to take a walk with no particular goal in mind. I want to have ears to hear, eyes to see, and to get lost observing a scene. I want to stop myself from living life to the fullest. It's only a waste. We lose our concentration. We go from one life to another, one country to another, one lover to another. We lose perspective. We're never really present.

I'm afraid of having a life, any kind of life. My life? I invent it.

I moved to America to play "American," like a kid playing Indian
or cowboy—I have no preference. I've had a hundred and sixty-
six jobs and I'm writing about the hundred and sixty-seventh
one. I'm not involved. I'm having an affair, and I keep my eyes
open. I don't want to be hurt. I don't need to expect anything.

What could be more suitable than ennui for someone "afraid of
having a life, any kind of life?" The more this student wrote, the
more she recognized how perpetual drifting perfectly served her
subconscious desire *not* to "do," as well as to exact revenge on her
father. With this awareness, she could begin to see, not only that
ennui had no power over her, but as its creator, she could transform
it into creativity, ardor, or manifestation whenever she felt ready.

Such realizations build increasing self-confidence. As we gain
perspective about how our desires serve us, we simultaneously gain
the power to manifest them and the wholeness to preserve them.

What I Resist Persists

Assignment: Part 1. List twenty-five things—people, situations, activities—you generally resist. List each one as a complete sentence or statement.

Example: I resist responsibility, stability, comfort, and
throwing anything at all away. I resist people who tell me what
to do, especially my mother who wants to create me in her
own image, but doesn't see that I am completely different, or
exactly the same striving to be completely different. I resist
savings accounts, certificates of deposit, and individual retirement accounts. I resist budgeting myself, limiting myself, any
type of constriction or restriction. I resist bras and shaving my
underarms. I resist anything that clings to my waist and
makes me self-conscious. I resist resisting, saying no, moder-

ation, and the kids in *Little House in the [Big] Woods* who licked their candy canes slowly and made them last all day while the younger children bit theirs and lamented afterwards. I resist the third little pig who built his house out of bricks. I resist crisply painted four bedroom houses with a light out front and children sleeping soundly in their beds while the parents stay up watching late night television.

I resist flirtatious men with egos like the necks of a lizard, red and fanned out, but just a thin piece of skin that can fold away into nothing, as he cries a truly heartfelt cry that I never guessed was there. I especially resist Leo men, my dad, Bill Clinton, and C's dad. Suave, extravagant, weasely, and arrogant. I resist exercise, washing my hair, showering, brushing my teeth, washing the toilet, and taking out the trash. I resist calling T. back whenever she calls me, and I resist the tact that is so necessary to placate my Sagittarian piercing honesty. I resist listening to A., to finding any humor, delight, or entertainment in any of the stories he tells over and over in various versions depending on the audience.

Part 2. Circle the five items you resist most.

Part 3. Write an individual scenario for each item in which you resist it to the most exaggerated degree imaginable. This is assisting the resistance. If you are a clean freak, become totally anal and obsessive: Your house becomes a sterile laboratory where you serve drinks only in Pyrex flasks heated over Bunsen burners and the air-conditioning is set at a permanent fifty-five degrees.

Part 4. Reverse it. Write what your life would look like, sound like, and feel like if you totally gave in to debt, illness, laziness, clutter, self-indulgence, loneliness, addiction, on whatever you most fear.

For example, if you resist paying bills, write a scene in which they stack up so high that you can only reach the top of the pile with a ladder, which you can't find because the electricity has been turned off for nonpayment and there are no lights and the line of bill collectors outside your door extends into the next county and looks like something out of Dr. Seuss. In the following example, the student who, in a previous exercise described how she resisted throwing anything away, surrendered to her resistance in the following piece of writing.

Example: I am the ultimate pack rat. Just like my mother, I throw away nothing that could possibly be reused. Shelves all over, but who needs 'em. There are floors and countertops and corners. Pile every bit in. Everything has a purpose. Waste not. Want not. I want everything . . . and more!

I can't get into this. I hate this. A pack rat storing endless clutter. Piles and piles of papers from college, from work, my writings, old receipts, greeting cards, Tupperware containers, glass jars with their labels carefully removed, McDonald's ketchup packets, unused napkins from Taco Bell, used pieces of tin foil, bits of thread, sundry buttons—boxes of them— knick knacks, old magazines, and shelves and shelves of books, borrowed, stolen, or bought with the best of intentions.

Then there's Mom's junk! I don't even want to think about it—a mirror of what I could be. She actually scares me into clutter sobriety. I stay up all hours night after night surrounded and immobilized by all the stuff, stuff, stuff! Just like in third grade when Mrs. Stormont moved me to the back of the room where all the clutter around my desk wouldn't trip anyone. Maybe I could get rid of the junk mail before Mom sees it. I could put it at the bottom of the trash. But she'd find out and dig for the coupons/flyers/community

SIX CLASSIC PRINCIPLES OF TRANSFORMATION   71

newspapers/even the Jewish Journal (and she's not even Jewish)!

_____

After writing your polar extremes, you will notice the similarity in their energy. Observation neutralizes that energy's intensity and restores a *dis*-passion, an antidote to the negativity that fueled that intensity. In place of the negativity, passion, rather than desperation, ignites. A terra firma is created from which insight, rather than impulse, explodes.

What You Acknowledge Increases

THE SECOND PRINCIPLE of Transformation balances the great measure of shadow work that is key to this process. Just as the shadow must be recognized and digested in order for affirmations to take root, positive thoughts and actions must be acknowledged in order for them to flourish. Remember, the subconscious mind is purely literal. Whatever our conscious minds say, the subconscious accepts as literal truth in its most extreme degree. The credit and support we give ourselves feeds our consciousness, expanding its positive effects. Energy and creativity are mutually reinforcing. Anger, guilt, jealousy, grief, and revenge dissipate constructive energy. Acknowledgment generates creativity and growth. Writing out acknowledgments directs them to our subconscious, where they are integrated. This is power.

Here are examples of some students' acknowledgments, written in the same spontaneous way:

- I acknowledge my willingness to nourish myself—both physically and creatively.

- I acknowledge that my wife is the center of my life.

- I acknowledge the hard work it took for the two of us to get here.

- I acknowledge I have finally granted myself time for self-exploration.

- I acknowledge that my writing is up to me.

- I acknowledge that I am searching. Not for an answer, but for a solution—a simple and elegant solution that will free me and not hurt others. I am searching for the freedom to choose gain, to give myself perspective. The freedom to see clearly. The freedom to take a risk.

Here is what a student who feared he was coming to the end of his creative career acknowledged:

Today I completed a project I conceived fourteen years ago. I did sketches about ten years ago and then a year and a half ago I decided to carry them through to completion. But I knew I could do this only if I mastered use of the computer.

I studied the books, I made mistakes, I asked questions of accomplished friends and professionals. I began feeling literate, then competent with the computer. Once I completed the final corrections and alterations on all five designs, I reduced the images small enough to look at them all together, spread out across the screen. Their wealth of details kaleidoscopically co-alesced into what looked like jeweled bracelets on black velvet. It was breathtakingly beautiful. "Here it is," I thought, "my doc-torate in computer illustration!"

I am as much relieved as thrilled to have completed this art-work because it has been such a long and complicated task. So many details. So many times it felt as if computer crashes or my own fear of completion, masked as perfectionism, were going to keep me from fulfilling my goal. But I redid each design time and again until it felt like music.

When I started this project I was fifty-eight years old and nearly paralyzed by my fear of losing it, of abandoning my own dream. Now, having turned sixty, I know I have as much talent, skill, stamina, and as many ideas as I did when I was working in New York during my "heyday." Only this time, I was my own client, my own art director, creating what the universe creates through me!

What I Acknowledge Increases

Assignment: Complete a sentence that begins "When I acknowledge myself . . . " and keep writing for three minutes.

Example: When I acknowledge myself, I sense the opposite forces that work at me. While part of me is acknowledging myself for the magnificence of an accomplishment, a whole Greek chorus in my mother's voice chants, "You don't expect to make money at that, do you, dear?" Then my own mind joins in: "Maybe I've left out some crucial detail and the whole project is a bust." That's my current musical favorite.

In the end I am exhausted by my continual effort and seldom stand back from what I'm doing long enough to say, "You know what, you did good!" But on those rare occasions when I do, it feels great. I love it when I live up to my own standards.

Review: Were you more or less receptive to positive reflection than you anticipated? Did the positivity resonate as deeply as the fearful, angry, or other unsettling subjects you've written about? What part of your body is most *un*responsive to positive acknowledgment?

Assignment: Write a list first of things you acknowledge about yourself, then about those people closest to you, and finally, about those you work with.

What You Withhold Is Withheld from You

WITHHOLDING DERIVES FROM the belief that our love, attention, and/or resources will be squandered if we give them out. It can result in physical, emotional, and spiritual constipation. Withholding congests the energy around our hearts and limits the energetic responses that a healthy giving-and-receiving relationship exerts. When we withhold, we abandon the loving impulses we innately possess in order to punish others or to be accepted by them. In turn, what returns to us is inadequate. The more we withhold, the less we have. The tighter we withhold, the less we receive.

I asked one student, who persistently felt shortchanged by life to write about "short change":

The Bag of Short Change

It's hanging from my neck, a big mail bag like the one I carried in grade school (PS 200) to collect the bank books that held the petty small change being deposited by all us good little kiddies in our pathetic little accounts at the Dime Savings Bank of Brooklyn—not even Dollar Savings, for Chrissakes.

It's got leather caps at both ends that are strapped through the strap holders on each side of them and it's made out of thick, rough tough cloth, a fabric I can't name, but tough, rough, and scratchy, like carpet pile. And it's bigger than me. It flops from my neck and wrenches me from side to side as it bounces and scuffs along the floor and kicks up into the backs of my knees, almost knocking me over, sending me flying.

It's like Sisyphus's rock, because it never leaves me. I can never rid myself of the motherfucker, and it rubs my neck raw and leaves a dry lump of rawness in my throat, makes me thirsty, but I can never slake it (slake is a stupid word).

It makes me tired an irritable and cross—oh, so cross—and the lump in my throat feels like it feels when you're sad, very sad, in an angry kind of way, a mourning kind of way, like someone died.

What's in the Bag?

Lots of accounts, that's what. Bank books, books of account, scores kept, scores to be kept, scores settled, so many unsettled. It is like the bag that held the bank books of the good little children, good little me, I was, they aren't, they weren't, it goes on still.

I watch what they do, file it away, carry my files around in my bag, this bag so big and getting bigger by the day, the hour, the freakin' minute, for goodgodsakes. There are rocks in there too, but they clink like metal—how can that be? Maybe it's coins, big coins so heavy to carry, the fucking short change. I'm resisting the metaphor, the image, the obvious, it's all so heavy, so cumbersome, so hard so heavy so tiring to carry, but what can I do? What in fucking heaven's name can I do? It goes on and on and on and on, goes on still, forever it seems, mustn't get carried on a false tide of literariness, I might be circling around the flame, putting wagons in a circle, something like that because the image of what's inside there won't come clear now. I do not know or will not tell.

"You've got a need to be outraged," said the Chicago shrink as we drove around St. Maarten. I loved him I think, took to him instantly, his history was identical to mine so I knew he *knew*, he *knew*! He *knew*!

Still circling I think. What's really in there? The books of account, that's right, but not enough.

In another example, one student observed her habits of withholding time and money:

Alone I expand. I have the capacity to waste a lot of time, and this waste is bliss. I feel eternal. There is plenty of time for me when I'm alone.

When I am in a relationship, I become mercantile in regard to time. I'm more attached to it, but it no longer feels abundant. I stop owning it. I stop wasting it. I allocate it . . . in the best way I can imagine. A little bit here for my lover, a little bit here for my work. A little here for writing. There for shopping. Here for my errands.

When it becomes really unmanageable, I start cutting time into pieces, like Lisa's pizza slices. I eat time and, naturally, don't digest it. I lose the ingredients of life. I stop being a cook. My time no longer belongs to me, or at least it no longer feels that way.

I wake up sad. I know I must get on the phone and feed the beast of love with news about myself, even though I am empty, even though I have no words to say, just a big headache. Somehow I must manifest my presence. I must give and receive.

I want to faint. Time becomes a kind of merchandise that cannot even be traded for money. I give it away so much. If it were mine I would probably be very wealthy.

Love is a dog that needs to be walked three times a day.

What I Withhold Is Withheld from Me

Assignment: Complete a sentence that begins "No, no, no, you can't have my . . . " and keep writing.

Example: No, no, no. You can't have my . . . I don't want to fill in the blank! I don't want to write about withholding because I am ashamed of it. I see other people whom I admire as giving, whereas I am always hoarding. Watching the clock, my refrigerator, my wallet, my energy. I suffer from a feeling of scarcity—the fear of destitution always lurks. I see myself as an old, toothless woman hiding under a bridge because I didn't withhold enough.

I broke up with Doug because he washed out his baggies and watered down the dish detergent—traits I now admire. He was the only man I knew who could live on and support two children on $23,000 a year and even take me to the movies occasionally, and still save money. Yet he was generous with me—especially emotionally. And I am always withholding, judging, and hoarding. And *still* finding myself with next to nothing.

Assignment: Assist the resistance. Write out a scene in which you win the lottery and spend everything on yourself alone. You give nothing to anyone. What exactly would you do with the money? How does pure self-indulgence make you feel? Who would be most disappointed in your lack of sharing? Does this please you or make you sad?

Review: How did writing this assignment make your body feel—did you notice congestion anywhere as you were "withholding?" Was writing about withholding your fortune hard or easy? Write about squandering your fortune now and see how your feelings compare.

———————

As you use your writing to practice withholding and releasing—food, sex, money, time, affection—the models for your behavior will resound. You will also recognize how you have chosen to interpret their consequences. This interpretation is your subconscious definition of divinity. These are your feelings about how the universe—and your Creator—treats you.

All Perception Is Projection

The tension between our old "reptilian" brain and our
new brain, between our limbic system and our neocortex, between our primitive urges and our cognitive
mind—all metaphors of our own invention—is at the
essence of being human. Perhaps this is why we watch
with such interest the behavior of others around us.
We realize that in everyone we see ourselves.

—ABRAHAM VERGHESE, M.D.

BELIEVING IS SEEING. What we see is what we believe we
see. Therefore, our perceptions of ourselves and the world derive
from within. What we perceive is simply the mirror on which we
project our "in-sights," consciously or unconsciously. This principle
extends not only to our perceptions of other people but also to our
immediate environment (including our pets and neighborhood), our
larger environment (social, political, and professional communities),
and to the world at large.

A hopeless perception of the world mirrors a hopeless view of ourselves. An angry perception of our colleagues echoes intense self-
judgment. Disappointment in people in general reflects hostile
self-regard. In the same way, acceptance and admiration toward others mirrors our own self-acceptance and self-possession.

One of my students, a psychologist who specialized in treating
mania, identified a source of her own chronic unease by recognizing her unconscious desire to emulate her patients. "Their stories
flew around my head in a charismatic way," she wrote. "These
patients were beautiful, by and large, *especially* when they were
manic. They were creative, laughing one moment and then
snarling the next. They fascinated me, for they were actresses,
anorexic models, scrupulous and obsessive housewives, brilliant
lawyers and physicians, men and women. I sat rooted to my

chair—assessing, treating, rehabilitating, scattering hope while recommending treatment. I sat rooted to my chair—wanting to fly on their wings."

Healthy projections are those that affirm our oneness. Unhealthy projections express a belief in separation. Because what we acknowledge increases, awareness of our projections increases our power to create. The more conscious we grow, the less personally we take the world and the more personally we take Creation. Once we understand the nature of our own reflection, we can truly see ourselves and others.

Whatever I Perceive Is a Projection of Myself

Assignment: Write about how you don't believe this principle for a second, how the world is what is it, and you are what you are, and there is no such thing as a blank slate.

Example: "All perception is projection"—what the hell does that mean? *Projection! Perception! Perception! Projection!* Chug chug chug chug bibbity-bobbity-BOO! It don't mean a thing (if it ain't got that swing) (Ain't got the ring.) (That thing.) (That cling.) (That ring-a-ding-ding.) "All perception is projection" could just as easily be "All projection is perception," which actually seems more . . . *accurate* to me. Because otherwise we can never be said to see/feel/understand correctly since everything we seefeelunderstand is merely a construct of our own inner world imposed upon the outer, but having no (not necessarily, anyway) no connection to that which it seeks to explain/analyze/illuminate.

. . . Whew! Pretty heavy, eh? Pretty damn philosophical-metaphysicalanalytical—and all that. Jazz.

I don't like being told that everything I seefeelunderstand is false and reflects nothing more than my own (essentially pathetic) little ego life. It feels like I'm being accused of lying (although that may be my projection, eh?)—and I hate—repeat: *hate*—to be called a liar! Also, I don't believe (don't, don't don't!) that we are incapable of seeing truth (*the* truth) plainly, with the faculties we've been given. That would make the world—the universe—life—ultimately unknowable; would comdemn us all to the prisons of our rocky selves, exiles all on some barren inner Elbas, without any hope of grace.

* * *

What I Hate About Others

Assignment: List the personality traits in others that most irritate or anger you. Make each statement a full sentence.

Example: I hate people who are pompous and pretentious. I have no patience for people who are inept. I can't stand people who are constantly distracted. I can't tolerate people who are always late. I hate people who are lazy. I could kill people who are inconsiderate. I am disgusted by people who are cheap. I have no sympathy for people who are forgetful.

Review: What traits appeared most? Who in your childhood exemplified these traits?

Assignment: Write a scene in which *you* embody the most aggravating of all these traits. What would you look like? How would you sound? How would others react to you? How would you feel about yourself—diminished or more powerful, ashamed or regretful, proud or indifferent? How is it that you knew these characteristics so well?

* * *

Contagion

Assignment: Write about contagion—your fear of it or your lack of fear of it. When did you first feel "dirty?" Write about cleanliness and how important it is or isn't to you.

Review: Did you recognize any connections between your thoughts and your actions? Who in your family holds beliefs about these subjects that are most like yours? Whose are the most opposite?

Assignment: Make a list of your heroines and heroes. What are the qualities you admire about them? When did you first admire each of these qualities in someone? Do you feel you are strong or weak in them?

———

As you recognize how this principle works in all aspects of your life, you will gain increasing objectivity. You will be able to distinguish between your own projections and the "actual" attributes of the subjects that mirror your projections. With this growing ability to see objectively, you will also gain self-trust.

You Get Not What You Want, but What You Believe

OUR BELIEFS, NOT our desires, determine what we manifest and, once having manifested them, whether or not we sustain them. When our subconscious beliefs differ from our conscious desires—that is, when we are not psychologically aligned—we generate confusion and frustration rather than fulfillment. And when we do succeed in manifesting what we want, any contradictory subconscious beliefs will ensure that our manifestations don't last for long. The subconscious message—that we don't deserve or need or qualify for our manifestations—will sabotage any long-lived fulfillment.

I once had a student who, after two failed marriages and numerous other unsuccessful romantic relationships, told me how "completely determined" he was to make his newest relationship succeed. I admired his attitude but, knowing that determination is an act *only* of the conscious mind, I also pondered what I surmised was still a rocky road ahead. For this student had probed only superficially at his beliefs. He had resisted any deep examination of the impact on his choices and behaviors of his adolescent physical and sexual abuse. I knew that regardless of how much determination he exerted, his subconscious self-loathing of his sexuality would inevitably undermine his new relationship—and the next and the next.

One student who claimed he wanted "justice" in his interactions perpetually received punishment and alienation instead. The more he explored his subconscious through writing, however, the more he recognized that punishment was exactly what he believed he deserved—and was therefore what he generated. Here is how he came to see this:

> I feel such rage and frustration. Why can't they see that I am powerful because I am right! They don't understand. Where can I go with this? Why does it feel so bad? I want to punish everyone around me when I feel bad, which is most of the time— well, much—of the time.
>
> I am beating my head against the wall. My guts run out. See what you've done to me? Thou sayest the Lord? And people come running. I want everyone to apologize to me for what I have suffered. And I want them to soothe my fevered brow. No, I don't know what I want. My desperation is my power. The gut churning, skin flailing, railing, smashing and fearful—everyone in my path so fearful.
>
> I don't want to apologize. I want to smash, punish, rail, hurt,

bruise, destroy everything in my path. I want to rise like Atlas, like a Titan, summoning my slaves, who must bow to me and thank me for my presence—and is it my presents? And now, lust for me and lust for life. I want power. My desperation is my power. I causeth myself to lie down, and when I rise up, it shall be a sign upon my door and charity shall never wane from the earth. It is my badge, my salvation, my desperation. It gets me what I want.

I causeth people to bow down to me and maketh me whole—an asshole.

I Get Not What I Want, but What I Believe

Assignment: Write a list of ten things that would make you feel obligated in any way to anyone.

Example: I would feel obligated if I were to accept financial help from P, advice from M, help moving from Evan and George, help with the kids from M, help with my work from Grace, and help with my relationship from M. I would die if I had to ask anyone to help me deal with my financial condition. It would be just too embarrassing and I'd never be able to repay them.

Assignment: Write a list of the ten things you want most.

Example: I want a committed relationship. I want a partner I can rely on. I want sex and money. I want to be free of struggle. I want rest, lots of rest. I want recognition for my work. I want a vacation. I want someone to shop and cook for me. I want a new car.

Review: Reread both assignments, keeping in mind how your feelings of obligation, for one, interfere with manifestation. Consider what other subconscious feelings might be sabotaging your fulfillment (e.g., distrust, penury, fear of looking foolish or greedy, fear of undermining your parents or surpassing your partner).

———————

Remember that your subconscious is strictly "obeying orders." What the conscious mind interprets as sabotage, the subconscious perceives as service. The more you recognize your subconscious beliefs, the more clearly you will see how they defeat—or support—your fulfillment. Once your beliefs and desires are fully aligned, manifestation is inevitable.

What You Give Out Is What You Want Most

All the giving I do is helpful and supportive. But how is it that no one could know what I need? I've always been too afraid to ask.

—ARLENE HUYSMAN, PH.D., writing student

OFTEN THE GIFTS we receive reflect more of the giver's tastes and interests than our own. Likewise, when we fall in love with a gift we intend for someone else, it's usually because we ourselves would love to have it. Or when we do something philanthropic, it is often because we have benefited at some time from another's charity or because a need we perceive "out there" is a projection of our own unconscious or unarticulated needs. This does not mean our philanthropic impulses are any less valid. It only means that by recognizing our projections, we gain clearer understanding of the source of our impulses.

With this writing process, we gain the ability to tell ourselves the truth about the presence or absence of our own altruism. We learn to distinguish between selflessness and self-fulfillment. We gather the courage to honestly say, "I want this for myself" or "I do this for myself."

What I Give Out Is What I Want Most

Assignment: Complete a sentence that begins "If I just give out more . . . " and keep writing.

Example: If I just give out more . . . care to others, then maybe someone will . . . care about me? God, isn't it the truth. The ultimate caretaker I am. And I am fabulous. There is none better. Not only can I take care of family, but friends, lovers, co-workers, even strangers. Oh yes, I will help you. It's a small price to pay for a great return. But how much more time, how many more conflicts, how many more triangles to be taken care of before . . .

Before what? It's too hard, too tempting, no, too hard to even utter.

So, haven't I given enough already! And half the time those ungratefuls, yes, ungratefuls, I know you don't want to believe it, but it is so. Those ungratefuls have never appreciated you! What do you think, that someday if you keep taking care of them, bending, breaking to exhaustion, then someone, possibly not even someone you've helped, will do the same for you! There, I uttered it.

Assignment: Write a list of the most unappealing gifts you ever received. Describe the worst in exaggerated detail.

Example: I got the world's ugliest afghan as a baby present—it was orange, olive green, and white with black edging.

And when I thanked the relative for her "lovely gift" . . . she made me another one!

I got file folders and bookkeeping supplies for my birthday. I hate practical gifts! I want jewelry, extravagances, things I can do without and wouldn't get for myself.

I got dolls. I hated dolls. I named the blond doll Beatrice because it was a name I detested.

I got dresses that looked like nothing I would ever, ever wear. Short-sleeved prints with fitted waists that demurely covered the knee. Always in bright colors, lovely colors, happy colors. They looked like they belonged on a nice Jewish girl who went to Hadassah meetings and wanted to marry a dermatologist.

Review: How did these gifts reflect the interests or tastes of the givers?

Example: My mother really wanted a highly social, civically involved daughter who would delight in community work and charity work and dating nice Jewish boys. Instead she got a ranting, raving fag hag who takes her clothes off for artists, who ran off and married a cowboy, and now lives like a recluse.

Assignment: Make a list of ten things you give out most— from sympathy to food to money to advice.

Example: I give money to the religious community and to everyone who comes to my door in need. I'm always feeding my friends, strangers too, for that matter. I give out advice, plenty. Look to me for help, that's my anthem. Lean on me, that's what I'm here for.

Review: How important are these things to *you*?

Example: Lean on me . . . bullshit! Everybody's a therapist. Lean on me, but when do I get to lean on you? I can lean on no one but myself. I am the only one who will support me. No one will say, "Here dear, here's the money to go to college." Or, "Oh, you're short this month. Here's $5,000. Don't pay me back. Lean on me."

Actually, I can lean big time, but I am afraid to. Leaning has big repercussions. You owe your life to them. There is always a price to pay. Too big, too big for whatever it's worth. I'm safer giving out.

———————————

We do not fully possess a belief until we consciously and non-judgmentally acknowledge it. Ambivalence between the conscious and subconscious about what we want produces doubt. Doubt generates erratic energy—disharmony that leads to dis-integration. It leaves us bereft of the very things we want or need.

Preservation of our creations requires wholeness—an integration of subconscious, conscious, and metaphysical belief. By writing daily and practicing the Six Principles—through observation, reflection, and these exercises—your transformation will accelerate.

The more you weave together the infinite aspects of your being, the more harmonious—and powerful—you grow. By doing this work, you *always* come away from the page understanding more about yourself. It activates your innate "enlightment mechanism." *You already have it. Use it.*

PART TWO

Healing: Uncensored Exploration

Pain is inevitable. Suffering is optional.

—SUSUN WEED, *Healing Wise*

CHAPTER FIVE

How Healing Works

You can think of healing as a power-sharing
arrangement between one's physiology, pathology,
psyche, emotional history, social context, medicines,
healers, and gods.

—MARC IAN BARASCH, *The Healing Path*

*W*e do not create, or even learn, by conscious concentration alone. The mind is not an instrument distinct from the body it inhabits and from that body's
surrounding environment. It communicates freely and
profoundly with the noncerebral anatomy, via both the
nervous system and the cardiovascular system. It can
receive powerful stimuli from outside events, both
great and small. Its various structures of language
make it an organic part of culture, of history. The

mind feeds on all these sources, yet transcends them

in its ability to modulate and focus their input.

—ROBERT GRUDIN, *The Grace of Great Things*

THE HEALING PROCESS is an idiosyncratic manifestation of physical, emotional, and spiritual energies, as unpredictable and individual as it is exquisitely organized. It can begin at any site of mind or body and at any point in the cycle of Creation and disintegration. Any "hole" in our well-being—whether physical, emotional, or spiritual—leaks life force from our whole being. By restoring any aspect of our being, we increase our wholeness, that is, improve our health. In metaphysical terms, to make whole is to make holy, and to make holy is to heal.

"Healing is always certain. It is impossible to let illusions be brought to truth and keep the illusions," teaches *A Course in Miracles*. Acceptance of healing is an entirely different matter. If, subconsciously, sickness serves us, a sudden healing can precipitate intense confusion, depression, or an unendurably deep sense of loss. "Healing will always stand aside when it would be seen as a threat," says *A Course in Miracles*. "The instant it is welcomed—as a blessing and not a curse—it is there."

This view of healing even accepts that *we may not be ready*, for whatever reasons, to give up our problems or our pain. This writing process allows us to harbor our problems—to resist healing—as a matter of conscious intent. When we make our resistance conscious, we consciously evaluate its value. As long as our resistance remains subconscious, it remains active and intact. Awareness neutralizes and diminishes it. If this concept is not sufficiently clear to you, review in chapter 4 the first Principle of Transformation— "What you resist persists"—and write "My resistance protects me."

Eventually, as we write, we learn exactly where in our bodies unresolved emotions reside and what messages particular pains, discomforts, or other physical reactions are sending us. This awareness informs us about how we habitually project past feelings onto present situations and what our bodies do to protect us from feeling them.

The most common physical reactions I have observed in students who are addressing themselves to chronically unsettling subjects are shortness of breath, tightness in the throat and chest, and churning in the stomach. Typically, the more we concentrate or extend our focus on a subject, the more acute the response will grow.

There are two ways to consciously deal with emerging feelings: We can remain with the feeling, writing about it to see what thoughts the discomfort leads to, or we can acknowledge in our writing that we are not yet prepared to deal with that feeling. Not being able to physically or emotionally handle a subject is acceptable. It is not bad, wrong, or a failure of any kind. It is simply the truth of our position at that moment, a position that *can* change when we are ready to try it out on paper. For example, a student dealing with an eating disorder wrote, "I don't want to write about food anymore. I don't want to eat it or write about it. I must forgive myself first. This writing makes me want to cry. Cry at how sick I am of this possession and dispossession. I used to not eat, and then they made me eat. Now I can't stop eating. Or crying." By recognizing the truth and accepting it, this student began the primary step in her healing. The more she embraced her confusion, the easier it became for her to move through it.

Our Chaos Holds Our Medicine

And gradually it dawned on him, if a dawning can
take place in total darkness, that his life had con-
sisted of a run of rehearsals for a play he had failed

> to take part in. And that what he needed to do from
> now on, if there was going to be a now on, was aban-
> don his morbid quest for order and treat himself to a
> little chaos, on the grounds that while order was
> demonstrably no substitute for happiness, chaos
> might open the way to it.

—JOHN LE CARRÉ, *The Night Manager*

GIVEN THAT THE human organism is conceived out of the uncharted alchemy of sweat, saliva, and semen amidst a chaos of desire and surrender that leaves the skin electrified, the muscles spent, the tissues wet, and the mind stilled, is it truly so difficult to consider that the healing of this same organism might also derive from chaos? Delivered through pain, bathed in blood, we are initiated upon birth into the inherent messiness of life.

Conscious descent into the chaos of dis-ease initiates restoration from the dis-ease. *Conscious,* as always, is the key word. We have been wallowing in various degrees of various descents for most of our lives. To choose to dive into our own chaos, explore it, embrace it, and use its power is to affirm life with potency.

When one student began writing about "the worst experience of my life," he found that "my stomach contracted and my heart began to feel as if it were enclosed in steel—shut tight away from the world on all sides. I closed my eyes and tried to remember back as far as I could, to the first time I had felt that same blocked sensation in my stomach. I was four and a half, in the basement of my father's store where Buster, the teenage boy who worked for us, unbuttoned his pants and smiled at me. . . . "

We must learn to die to our fear, pain, grief, anger, jealousy, anxiety, or rage before we can resurrect into wholeness. Dancers learn that the only way to achieve elevation in a jump is to deepen their plié. In life as in dance or any form of creativity, and in healing as in birth, we must give ourselves over to descent before we can ascend.

Every Healing Experience Is Unique

It is first necessary to understand that all thoughts
and feelings are powerful agents of creative energy,
regardless of whether the thoughts are true and wise
or false and limited. Likewise, whether the feelings
are loving or hateful, angry or benign, fearful or peaceful, their energy must create according to their nature.
Thoughts and opinions create feelings, and both of
them together create attitudes, behaviors, and emana-
tions that, in turn, create the life circumstances.

—EVA PIERRAKOS, *Guide Lectures for Self-Transformation*

ALL TRULY EFFECTIVE healing traditions—ancient and con-
temporary, conventional and alternative—consider each and every
situation to be unique. Therefore, all possible treatments—from meditation to surgery—and all possible combinations of treatments—
including meditation *and* surgery—are viable. Many such traditions
also embrace the notion of finding the cure through the "poison." In
homeopathy, a school of medicine developed in the nineteenth cen-
tury, small doses of the toxin that is creating the illness are used to
build the resistance to defeat it. The modern principle of inoculation
works in a similar way. Chinese medicine works not by attacking the
illness but rather by restoring energy and balance, thereby fortifying
resistance.

All possible approaches to healing are viable because every story
is unique. In other words, anything that contributes to wholeness,
including dis-ease itself, can be considered healing.

It is important to understand that healing does not necessarily
mean that the physical body recovers from an illness. Healing can
also mean that the spirit has released long-held fears and negative
thoughts. This kind of spiritual release and healing can occur even
though the body may be dying physically.

CHAPTER SIX

Physical and Emotional Healing

Making my thoughts known, both to myself and
others, literally allows me to breathe free.

—HORTENSE LEON, writing student

Your biography becomes your biology.

—CAROLINE MYSS, PH.D., *Anatomy of the Spirit*

ILLNESS REPRESENTS A place where we are stuck in our story. Debt, dis-ease, and social, creative, and personal paralysis also represent places where we are stuck in our story. *When our attention is fixed on one aspect of our lives, we cannot create, only re-create.*

As our culture grows more obsessed with the appearance and physical condition of our bodies, we are increasingly bombarded with a parade of the newest in exercise, diets, remedies, devices, supplements, medications, applications, treatments, and procedures. Fortunately, as recognition of the power of inner exploration grows, even conventional medical communities are recognizing the correlation between inner strength and progressive well-being.

The restorative mechanism in the physical body thrives on unimpeded circulation—of blood, oxygen, and nutrients. Without complete circulation, toxins accrue, stagnation inaugurates putrefaction, and the physical system, poisoned, disintegrates. Thus, impeded or distorted circulation diminishes wholeness. Likewise, a flexible emotional anatomy is equally critical for the health of the psyche. Denial or attempted containment of uncomfortable or painful feelings produces emotional putrefaction that manifests in physiological expressions we call symptoms. Symptoms indicate the breaking down of a system's ability to adjust to disturbance or imbalance. If we look no further than the elimination of a symptom, we are ignoring its message. In other words, what we think we want to eradicate may be exactly what we need to focus on.

The writing process described in this book restores circulation of energy through the simple acts of observation and listening. The power generated by these fundamental acts promotes subconscious shifts, which lead to physical and emotional balance. Such healing requires *no external effort* to fix or change anything in or about your life. In fact, to attempt to fix a situation or to create change is to disrupt the innate subconscious mechanism for restoration.

The human body is a self-restoring organism at every level of biological organization, from DNA upward. Cells are made of molecules, which are made of atoms. As many as 95 percent of the octillion atoms in a healthy body are replenished every year. For example, the atoms in the skin are replenished every thirty days, and those in the stomach in less than one day. The red blood supply is replenished every 120 days, and the oxygen supply with each breath.

Studies have corroborated estimates by Franz J. Ingelfinger, M.D., former editor of the *New England Journal of Medicine,* which show that 75 percent of all illnesses brought to physicians are self-limiting. In only about half of the cases of the remaining 25 percent has medicine shown to be dramatically helpful. With these statistics, we can only conclude that modern medicine has profoundly underestimated the innate mechanisms of self-diagnosis, self-repair, and regeneration that are perpetually poised to become active within the human organism when the need arises.

While we may have conscious and subconscious reasons for suffering, we have no biological excuses for allowing ourselves to suffer—or perish—out of lack of awareness. Unlike primitive animals such as frogs, which have only one brain (the reptilian), humans actually have three: the reptilian, which activates fright or flight mechanisms; the mammalian, which governs emotions, feelings, and memory; and the neocortex, from which evolves cognition, expanded awareness, and the freedom to choose and act. This writing process activates the neocortex and generates awareness of memory embedded in the reptilian and mammalian.

Caroline Myss, Ph.D., author of *Why People Don't Heal, and How They Can* and *Anatomy of the Spirit,* explains in the latter book that "positive and negative experiences register a memory in cell tissue as well as in the energy field in the form of neuropeptides, which could be described . . . as thoughts converted into matter by the chemicals triggered by emotions. . . . The same kinds of cells that manufacture and receive emotional chemistry in the brain are present throughout the body."

Simply described, the cycles of the human organism work like this: Biochemistry produces the thought that stimulates the energy that generates the feeling that prompts the behavior that forms the external environment that reinforces the beliefs that promote the biochemistry and so forth. In *Anatomy of the Spirit,* Caroline Myss writes:

Every thought you have had has traveled through your biological system and activated a physiological response. Some thoughts are like depth charges, causing a reaction throughout the body. . . . Some thoughts are more subtle, and still others are unconscious. Many are meaningless and pass through the body like wind through a screen, requiring no conscious attention, and their influence upon our health is minimal. Yet each conscious thought—and many unconscious ones—does generate a physiological response.

According to Myss, illnesses or dis-eases (caused by other than environmental and genetic factors) are a result of negativity infused into the natural cycle. They develop as a consequence of attitudes and behavioral patterns that we do not realize are biologically toxic until they become so. To create dis-ease, negative emotions have to be dominant. Furthermore, illness accelerates when we recognize the negative thought to be toxic yet permit it to thrive in our consciousness anyway.

Carl Jung believed that disease begins when a personality's story is denied. Similarly, I view the symptom as the initial note in a story written on the body by *suppressed* responses to family, religion, and society. Healing, on the other hand, results from experiencing the *fullness* of our humanity, from the acceptance of flaws, imperfections, confusion, mistakes, and aberrations. Healing occurs when we allow chaos and the emotional blood and mess it produces to move through our lives rather than keeping these subconsciously buried. *Healing begins when we rediscover our story.* Only with this rediscovery can we retell the story, expose its deeper roots, uncover new meanings, and create an ending different from the self-fulfilling prophecy that has been directing our unconscious script.

Our Untold Stories Run Our Lives

Of the forty-two classes at Harvard whose course descriptions include Freud or psychoanalysis, no

course on Freudian psychoanalysis is offered in the
psychology department or in the medical school. All
were listed in the humanities and most in literature.

—ALAN A. STONE, M.D.,

"Where Will Psychoanalyis Survive?", *Harvard Magazine*

ALL PSYCHOANALYTIC THERAPY, regardless of the specific
school of practice, begins with a developmental historical account
of the individual, that is, with his or her story. Even as the academic
field becomes more "scientific" and psychiatry becomes more biological, psychoanalysis thrives in popular culture, where, as Dr. Alan
Stone, former president of the American Psychiatric Association,
explains, "it has become a kind of psychological common sense, as it
has in every other domain where human beings construct narratives
to understand and reflect on the moral adventure of life."

Allowing yourself to write freely, without judgment or censoring,
enables you to simultaneously recognize old stories buried in the
subconscious that have outlived their service, to liberate yourself
from their spell, and to use the rich resources of the subconscious to
create new stories.

Consider how this student resolved her lifelong insomnia by
observing her resistance to "being anchored":

A good night's sleep. What's that? Well, I was an insomniac until
I met my real anchor. I thought that anchors rooted you, held
you down, didn't allow you to move, were millstones around the
neck. But I've found through being, living with, and trusting this
partner, that anchors are something else altogether.

My anchor allows me to stop, rest, regroup, retool . . . to
sleep, perchance to dream. My dreams comfort me as I lie next
to him—feeling the safety of not flying off in the wild blue yon-
der—that place I was afraid of in all those years I couldn't sleep.

I'm no longer afraid of sleeping. But old habits die hard. All I have to do each and every night now is tell myself, "I can trust this man." Then I can sleep. And, eventually, it will be a good night's sleep.

We lift the spell of an old story through the act of direct observation. We release the power of old stories that keep us stuck and unhappy by foregoing judgment. Secrets breed deceit. Their toxicity is purified by acts of nonjudgmental disclosure—even if that disclosure is only to ourselves through writing.

In the following writing examples, a student, locked in her old "helpless little girl" story explores it, inflates it, and, by withholding judgment, allows a new image to evolve.

I am a helpless little girl. This is my secret. I can't plan the feeling—it appears whenever it wants to. It seems to have a life of its own. Right now I am a grown-up version. When the two of us are together, I like her a lot. When I give her attention, like I'm doing now, she is not me. I am I, and I am fine, and so is she.

It's when I am out to lunch that I become her and then I have a terrible time with me. Going to lunch is such a grown-up thing to do. I love it until I get there and have to talk grown-up talk. I get so bored and feel helpless. I want to run out and push elevator buttons like Eloise or race through fields of wild flowers or I don't know what. I was going to say nurse at my mother's breast, but, yuk, I don't mean that.

My feelings are so little—even the big, booming powerful ones. When I talk them or write them they are teeny tiny. I think that is called shame. What a shame. Shame on me. Sing a song of shame and skip rope. My heart skips. I am nervous.

I am smaller still. I feel I am going downhill. This is no longer fun. I am not in the sunshine. Fun turns to fear. My chest is pounding. My heart is filled with a terrible sadness and fear. In my house no one rests. My mother screams, my father screams back. I am too scared to sleep. I am alone in my skin, my bed is too big, and the darkness is everywhere. I am alone alone alone and too afraid to cry. Helpless, little, and bad as well. I am a bad little good girl.

I feel better now, but my heart is still pounding. . . .

This little girl lost becomes the giant nervous wreck of the world. I fall asleep instead of falling apart. When morning comes, I awaken to the singing of birds and I am happy the night is done. I notice that I am now a giant, large, gargantuan balloon—bright yellow like the sun and with big, floppy red ears. My nose is big with orange and blue polka dots. My new name is Fearless Phyllis. I float in the Macy's Thanksgiving Day parade.

Everyone laughs as I wiggle and shake and tremble. But I am a wreck. People are not taking me seriously. I decide to become a bigger and bigger balloon. Now people are amazed. I am Awesome Fearless Phyllis. Children run to see me. They love me, they touch me. Fearless Phyllis balloon dolls are sold by the millions. They shake, they twitch their eyes and they stutter. They float along the ceilings of children's rooms. They glow in the dark, and the children know they are not alone. Children who used to be afraid are never afraid again.

Once you no longer identify with your old character in an old story, its power is gone. You are free to play the fool, the clown, the hopeless romantic, the snob, or any other role with joyful abandon because the former character no longer has any hold on you. You have embraced it in your literature, revised, and released it. You erased your shadow by inflating it into a massive cloud that, of its own accord, drifts away.

The Mind-Mouth Filter

Assignment: Write out, word for word, a recent unpleasant conversation, recording not only what you and the other person said but also what your mind was saying as you spoke.

Example:

HIM: Hi, how are you?

ME: Fine, thanks. (My God, who dresses these people—you'd think *someone* would insist on *some* standard of professionalism. Don't they realize what kind of impression they make?)

HIM: I'm afraid your order isn't ready.

ME: But I brought it in three days ago! (Jesus Christ, these people are the dumbest, most ill-organized bunch of losers. I was a total jerk to come here in the first place. How the hell do they stay in business!)

HIM: I'm sorry. We can deliver it if you want.

ME: Big deal! You told me it would be ready. I specified this date. I want my order! (This always happens, always, always, always. I get screwed and it's never my fault. What the hell kind of system is this!) You know, you guys ought to install a different system—you need one that . . .

Review: What did you experience in your body as you were writing? Did you notice any change of feeling in your writing hand when you came to uncomfortable parts of the conversation? How different was the monologue in your head from the one that came out of your mouth?

Assignment: Write out the same scene in which the filter between your mind and your mouth is inoperative and you actually speak the words in your head.

Example:

HIM: Hi, how are you?

YOU: I feel like shit, and looking at you in those sloppy clothes, all ungroomed, is making me feel worse. Isn't there some sort of dress code in this place? Don't you have any idea of the impression you make?

HIM: Well, fuck you dude! Now what exactly do you want?

ME: I want my order. I brought it in three days ago.

HIM: I'm sorry. It's not ready.

ME: What! You told me it would be ready. I specified this date. You're just like the other incompetents in this city. You don't know how to dress, you can't even speak decent English, and you can't get my work out! This always happens, always, always, always. I get screwed and it's never my fault.

HIM: Oh yeah?

ME: Yeah! Now what about my order, asshole!

HIM: I told you, dude. It's not ready. We can deliver it later, but I can't give it to you now.

ME: You people are all the same! Raving incompetents! I'm the only competent person in this whole goddamned city! Go back where you came from, why don't ya!

HIM: Because where I came from disappeared in a bombing along with my whole family.

ME: Oh, well, that's no excuse for incompetence.

HIM: And there's no excuse for your mouth, so why don't you just take your order and get the hell out of here.

ME: How dare you speak to a customer like this! Get me the manager!

HIM: I'm not getting your order, and I'm not getting the manager. But I am getting real sick of your face, and if you don't
  get it out of *my* face, I'm going to put a fist through it.
ME: Oh yeah?
HIM: Yeah! *Wham!*

Review: What happens or would happen if and when you
actually interacted like this in your life? In fact, this exaggerated version is the posture your subconscious sustains.

Liberating Our Literature

DIS-EASE DOES NOT germinate where self-expression is
fluid. The healing is in the telling, first to ourselves and then to the
world. Health results from recognizing our stories (all of them—our
family's, religion's, and society's, as well as those we've told ourselves
in order to survive), owning these stories completely, and releasing
them via the imagination.

What we withhold is withheld from us, and we cannot release
that which we do not recognize we are withholding. By writing, we
hear what we *do not* say as well as what we *do* say. We recognize
actions we subconsciously avoid and those we deliberately take in
order to avert our wounds. Writing allows us to heal our wounds by
observing how we hide them. Liberating our stories allows us to
reinvent them, to create a new personal literature that is nourishing
and uplifting.

A student whose late husband was a professional writer suppressed her own marvelous stories out of fear of comparison with
his. Once she stared writing, however, she discovered her enormous
ability to express herself in vibrant prose:

Begging for a Voice

Who the hell do I think I am? Sure I have stories, many of the same stories to tell that he did. But he had the vocabulary, he had the impeccable style. Shit, even when he dictated to his secretary, it was with full punctuation and capitalization and even little explanations for her of words she might not know. He would concoct something in his head for weeks and sit down and type it out perfectly, pages and chapters flowing without any need for a rewrite. I admired his abilities so much that I didn't dare write my own, even though there were so many stories rattling around in my head, I could hear them begging to be set down.

Now I realize I've been thinking about a particular story that was really on its knees begging for its voice, but that I thought too risque or risky to tell. When I started this class, I jumped right over that story and went to a safe and funny one—one of the many in my head, but by far not the most provocative.

I guess it's hard for me to tell those stories that reveal a different side of me, having spent my life trying to project the image of always doing what's right and responsible. Those begging for expression are the ones of love, underwater love, continental love, madness, schizophrenia, too many stories of anger and passion to come from a calm, patient, and well-behaved woman like me. Who would ever guess at the stories I have in me?

Liberating our literature opens doors to all manner of healing. It allows us to grow fearless about intimacy, to recognize underlying causes of suffering, to safely probe those causes, to alleviate their effects, and to fulfill ourselves confidently.

Fearless Intimacy

Live in the present fearlessly. Whatever is present,
take it to the end through your writing. The more
freely you write about your obsession, the quicker it
will depart.

—ALINA PANTERA, teacher

Acknowledging the truth, even the truth about our
fear, perhaps especially the truth about our fear, creates credibility.

—GERRY SPENCE, *How to Argue and Win Every Time*

THE MORE OUR feelings about ourselves are conflicted, the
more frightened we are of intimacy. Through writing, we grasp the
nature of our conflicts. As we vent on the page, we find ourselves
less distracted by peripheral issues and increasingly more focused
on the deeper sources of our fear. We learn, for example, that we're
not so much afraid of our current lover leaving as we are furious at
the parent who long ago abandoned us. Or that we actually feel less
hesitant about emotional commitment than of financial commitment. Or that it's not the other person we distrust, but ourselves.
With such insights, we can address the true issues rather than
resisting, blaming, or fleeing from close relationships that in some
way mirror our inner conflicts. Without this recognition, we simply
recreate our dis-ease in other contexts.

Here is an example: After her divorce, a student who came from
a highly orthodox religious family, marriage, and community found
herself as enslaved by her newly liberated status as she felt in her
previous life. Having left a world in which every aspect of her life
was precisely prescribed, she found herself lost in uncertainty and
self-doubt—about everything from social behavior to her own sexu-

ality. She had gone from being a virginal bride to an orthodox wife for twenty years and, at last, to being a "free" woman. Once "free," however, she felt terrified of the potential consequences of her untested liberty. Her writing revealed the source and depth of her fears:

A Babe, Bound

I'm 45 and divorced and I'm supposed to be a Babe now! Whose babe am I? Everybody seems so much more knowledgeable, so much more worldly—so much more. I don't even know when a man is interested in me, or, for that matter a woman!!

Fuck the world that split me in two! I feel like a cripple—so out of touch with my own needs. What do I want?

I feel so old, so old. I do not know about making peaceful choices. My life was dictated to me, and if I wanted something I had to rebel to do it my own way. Now I am free—free of a world that bound me with its doctrines and dogmas. But I *still* feel bound. I still feel caged—only now it is in a foreign world where I have no idea of the rules. Now I'm afraid of making choices, my own choices, choices based on my true needs. Is it because I don't know who I am outside my cage? I feel like a foreigner, trying to mimic the accent, but never really understanding the language.

Can I ever be a Babe in this new world? Is that what my sexist world taught me—that now I am the "forbidden fruit!" The Babe that sent Adam into expulsion and made Eve suffer the birth pains and cut the legs off the snake. All because she wanted to be someone else's Babe!

And then what? What if . . . what if it all weren't true? LIES!! You mean it's a lie? Have I been betrayed all my life? Have I been betrayed by someone else's idea of truth? What is my

truth?! What is a babe, anyway?! A quick fuck, an erotic seduc-
tion, a one-night stand? Babes don't last. They turn out to be
has-beens and end up dead in some cheap hotel!

Filled with such thoughts, would it ever be possible to have, let
alone enjoy, an intimate relationship? This student proceeded to use
her writing to try out different scenarios, allowing her imagination to
precede her into her new life. As she informed herself—mind and
body—of her fears and desires, she gained the balance to venture
forth.

Getting Close

Assignment: Complete a sentence that begins "Whenever I
get really close to another person . . . " and keep writing.

Example: Whenever I get really close to another person, I
get excited. Oh boy, someone to share my passions with, my
interests, my curiosities. I tend to idealize people. . . . I know
this about myself. To see their hearts and assume that there is
sanity there. God knows, I've enrolled a list of mighty self-
absorbed and self-destructive people in my life. Candy said,
"You fall in love too fast." Right, of course. I don't fall, I leap,
bungee jump without the bungee cord. Thrill to the fall and
then wonder why it takes years to recover.

Assignment: Write out a scenario in which you behave in an
intimate relationship in a manner completely opposite to your
typical pattern.

Example: I tried this last year with the lawyer. She was nuts
about me, and usually it's the other way around. As a matter of
fact, she behaved just like I usually do . . . and it sickened me. I
didn't want to be consumed by her. I didn't want to be part of

her already totally envisioned little drama. I didn't want to fit into her boring, wholly intellectual, uninspired life. I kept trying to give it a go. Give it a chance. God knows she was intense, persistent . . . qualities I usually admire. But she was also petty and passive/agressive and I knew that under that magnanimous shell lay a seething volcano of disappointment waiting to erupt. I didn't want to be around for the fallout.

OK, so I'm looking at *her*, not at myself. *Her* behavior, not mine. Yeah, yeah, where's the mirror? Well, first of all, to behave in an opposite manner, I wouldn't get swept away (boring, boring). I would chose someone steady, pleasant, even-tempered, not the intense ones I usually connect with (also boring). Someone who was enraptured with my music and the life of a musician, but who is sustained by her own passions, as well. (That has potential.)

Yeah, passion is a big deal. Sex is a big deal. This would be a woman who want to devote herself to real exploration, who isn't afraid. Maybe if *I'm* not afraid, I'll attract someone who isn't either. Now there's a novel thought.

––––––––––

Writing provides a place to explore past fears about intimacy as well as any and all future scenarios. It gives us a place to practice becoming exactly the kind of person we want to attract or keep, to be the kind of person we would want to surround ourselves with.

Recognizing Subconscious Causes of Chronic Problems and Pain

You will be able to read your body like a scripture.

—CAROLINE MYSS, PH.D., *Anatomy of the Spirit*

Sickness can actually be a result of *not* having symptoms. In *The Healing Path,* Marc Ian Barasch explains that "the symptom is a herald—or perhaps more accurately a harbinger—of a systemic pathology extending beyond the place it first appears, perhaps even beyond the body itself, into the family, the society, the environment. A symptom is more than an announcement—it is a collision of intersecting forces." Underlying every symptom, according to hypnotherapist Nicolas J. Mason, are three fundamental messages: first, that the channels for communication between the mind and body need to be cleared; second, that the meaning of the communication must be deciphered; and third, that balance must be restored among mind, body, and spirit.

Psychologically, a symptom may represent an attempt to throw off the deadening touch of the emotional past—a final effort before dis-integration ensues to both exorcise and express deep personal pain. The site of the symptom is often the place where the issues of transformation are focused most poignantly, most pressingly. When you write about your symptoms, you give them voice. You give yourself the opportunity to hear their message. Consider the story written by a student who suffered from chronic sore throat and laryngitis:

I awake voiceless from a night's tumultuous sleep. The imaginary—or were they real?—hands squeezed my neck as if to choke the very life out of me. Speak no more? Not I. This too shall pass and I shall speak, even as a jabberwocky, hoarse and raspy. Even if I have to use my toes to do it, I will speak! Breathe, pump, speak!

"Who the hell do you think you are?" my self-centered Daddy (can I call him that?) screamed when he heard I was going to sing in a state music competition. He grabbed me around the neck as if to choke the sweet, powerful, four-octave tenor voice out of my young boy body. Mother—not Mom or Mommy—simply stared as always, locked up inside her mind's safe and empty attic.

I'm twelve. My Daddy lost his leg when he was twelve. He'd thrown a bunch of grain—oats—at the hired hand who threw them back. And to avoid being hit, good ole Daddy (young, proud, foolish tease of a boy) jumped into the path of an oncoming car. The oats were sown, and we three very special boys had to live out the sins of our father: Be normal, average, not too special. Draw no attention to our Daddy, the richest and most powerful man in this fish bowl of a town, an amputee who had become the Great Pretender with the perfect, silent Stepford wife. No room for greatness in *this* family. No great sons, no great fathers. Everyone must look perfectly normal and stay silent.

"OK, Daddy, I promise. I promise not to sing sweet lyrical—slap! I'm sorry—music." Hate burns in my belly, and my fingers are crossed so tightly I can't breathe. I promise to look perfect (but not be perfect). I'll keep quiet and keep your secret, your dirty little secret! Secrets and lies. My tomb of deafening silence.

Those childhood years were not for the child in me, no, they were dead years. Just a vague, empty, lonely line to walk in silence. "I promise, Daddy. I promise." But I can't say it . . . because I'm silent.

Slaaasshhh. I'll cut you to death. I'll cut you away, my suffocating parents. You didn't want me. You just had me. Fuck it. I have been had. No more!

I will sing the Hallelujah Chorus, but not on your grave, even though you're dead. Dead silence. Dead calm. Dead away from me. But . . . can that be . . . music I hear? Music faintly resurrecting itself, faintly, but ever stronger. Overcoming me. Is that my voice? It sounds like an angel's. I'm sorry, did I say that?

Even when a condition is not wholly ameliorated by attitudinal change, a metaphysically enlightened view of that condition—a view that promotes willingness to alter beliefs and receptivity to change—enhances the healing process. Here, for example, is a student's observation of her seemingly simple and certainly common symptom—acid stomach.

The bitter taste in my mouth is not in my heart at all, but in my throat, above my stomach. I block, dismiss, bury, throw away some truth, some clue. The taste is bitter, a taste I now imagine my daughter knows all too well from her "eating disorder." Can I take it from her and *then* throw it away—the taste or the truth? Aha! The world gone sour.

I feel bitterness toward . . . I have no idea. Shall I go through a list and see what makes me throw up? Let's start with M. Seems a mean thing to do—such a sweet girl. How can I feel so bitterly towards my own daughter? How can it be?

Because I've sacrificed and worried and lived paralyzed by fear of doing something wrong, fear that she'll be a carbon copy of me—with my faults, my fears, my pain. How's that stomach now? Getting churned up!

Here is another student's observation of stomach pain:

Stomach aches, sick feelings, that icky sickness at the bottom of my stomach. It creeps into the rest of my body if I can't calm myself down. It grows unbearable. What do I do to make it better? Usually nothing. I just make it worse.

Why? Because I deserve to feel sick. I deserve to feel my entire body tighten. Then my chest and my heart cave, collapse like an imploding building.

On the outside no one can tell. Well, they didn't used to be able to. Lately, it's beginning to show. I must work on that. Never let anyone know I'm hurting. After all, I can handle anything—or so I thought. *Am I becoming weak, or am I just beginning to be alive?*

Recognition of the connection between their stomach conditions and their feelings of bitterness and self-judgment enabled these students to address their problems consciously. Rather than merely medicating their discomfort into numbness, they used it to lead themselves to awareness—and healing. Ultimately, one of these students wrote:

> At last I give to myself. I love deeply . . . can even love myself deeply. I'm learning to live for myself and thereby truly care for others. Care without sacrificing, care without making myself sick to my stomach—or ill at ease or sick with apprehension.
>
> I've learned how to allow those I've helped to care for themselves, to grow within themselves. Just like I am.

Utter Incapacity

Assignment: List the consequences to your family of your becoming totally incapacitated or dysfunctional. Write out a scene illustrating it.

Review: How does your degree of anxiety over this possibility correspond to the actual probability of this occurring? Who, besides you, would be affected most? Who would be affected least? Is this degree of anxiety typical of your concern of how the world views you? Who else in your family shares this type or degree of anxiety? What is your first memory of this anxiety?

As you grow aware, you know instinctively what to do and not do, what warrants action and what requires silence and study. By distinctly hearing the messages your symptoms offer, you gain knowledge of your body and the way your body/mind/heart works.

Alleviating the Effects of Specific Patterns of Thought and Behavior

Deep feeling is soul retrieval.

—ALINA PANTERA, teacher

HEALING REQUIRES RECOGNITION, acknowledgment, embrace, and expression. Writing gives us a means to recognize and acknowledge our beliefs, embrace our thoughts, and express our deepest feelings. Without such a process we cannot release our pain, fear, and toxicity. It is impossible to let go of that which we do not acknowledge, just as we cannot celebrate that which we do not embrace. Expression is vital to growth, wholeness, and healing.

Protecting Whom?

Assignment: Who would be most affected by your succumbing to your most persistent physical, mental, or financial condition? How would it affect them? How would it affect you?

Example: If I were to totally succumb (say 400 pounds worth!) to my obsession with food, my family would put me away. My brother has already offered to pay me to lose weight. I am the fattest of anyone in the family. I see how they look at me without saying anything. But no, I wouldn't do it. It's not worth it, not even to piss them off.

Review: What was the dominant feeling this writing expressed? Is it what you expected? The student who wrote the above piece, for example, expected to be swallowed with sorrow when she wrote about the possibility of her weight ballooning. Instead, she discovered how strong her anger was toward her family and how powerfully her weight served to avenge her.

Assignment: Write a scene in which your anger, despair, sorrow, or confusion has been resolved. What do you look like, feel like, and sound like, and how are your habits affected?

Passionate expression—within the sanctuary of your writing or art—transforms experience, no matter how long forgotten, deeply buried, or seemingly unacceptable. Transformational work, by its nature, has emotional, physical, and spiritual aspects. When you respond to the soul's longing, you grow full of feeling and the need to express your heart's desire.

Reliving Sensitive or Volatile Experiences Safely and Redirecting Their Effects

Once we make conscious our emotional needs, it's impossible to forget them. Once we become aware of the source of any unhappiness, we cannot expunge that awareness.

—CAROLINE MYSS, PH.D., *Anatomy of the Spirit*

WE NEED TO know if our attitudes or actions are costing us energy or enhancing our life. This writing process enables us to return to our wounds and touch, smell, poke, and even dig at them with diminishing apprehension. The safer we feel, the more we gain dispassion and an ability to clinically examine our wounds.

As we grow fearless about reliving on paper the confrontation, disappointment, or trauma that caused us so much pain, we can at last expose our wounds and treat them appropriately. Then we are free to heal. When we can freely write about our hate, terror, and pain, we can freely love. In the following example, a student "howls" unrestrained over her mother's abandonment:

Last night I woke up crying. I had dreamt I was dying of loneli-ness. It wasn't related to my husband or sexuality at all. It was feminine loneliness. The loneliness that comes with being bar-ren or feeling a lack of material bonds. It is a genetic loneliness.

I am PMSing and craving female bonding. The nurturing that comes from being female with another woman. Aching and yearning, shopping and dreaming, bitching and moaning together.

I miss the feminine bond I once had with my mother. She knew what women love. She indulged in feminine wildishness. The impulse to buy a fragrance or soft clothing. The need for fat and salt or rich sweetness. The depth of a fine, aromatic liquor or the drowning of senses in a cold beer. The searching for one's soul in the horizon of a tempestous ocean, or sitting out in a rainstorm until hypothermia sets in.

I miss these things—they are part of feminine madness. The hormonal surges leading to impetuous behavior. The weightiness of swelled breasts and uterine lining that harm, if not destroy, credit lines.

On days like today I feel I might never shower again. I can roll in filth and exult in the richness of dirt and stench. My womb is fighting against my will. It is torturing me in my dreams and water retention. By refusing to slough off my bloodied walls, it is increasing the tension of surfacing insecurities I refuse to face. My womb is creating a physical revolution against my will-ful, chemically imposed barrenness. Even the hair on my head is standing on end, my eyelids are heavy, and my mind is sluggish.

Today I hate my mother for depriving me of her company. As toxic as she is, I found comfort in her presence. She is smart and understands feminine mysteries. As much as she taught me about being a woman and what I've picked up on my own, she always added a new insight or created a new form of decadence.

Her perverse nature was pure bitch. Nothing is better than bleeding in her presence. She urged the blood down, affirming her own hatred of children. All children exist to bother her. Her own children existed to wrench her life and keep her from her dreams and aspirations. We ruined her art, her intellect, and robbed her of her physical freedom. She was burdened with the responsibilities of four other lives and robbed of her own. HA!!!

Blameless or Not?

Assignment: Return to the issue you wrote about in the previous exercise. Who have you considered blameless in regard to this condition? Write about them.

Example: It's funny. While everyone else in my family thinks I'm fat, my mother thinks I don't eat enough. I'm never hungry when I'm around her. She told me I was premature. . . . No wonder as a child I was underweight.

I'm crying. Just writing the word "fat" made me cry . . . and I thought that I was done with it! As the words flowed from my pen, I saw the image of that young girl—me—who was so afraid. I felt so sad for her that she would want or choose to starve herself to death. I feel some relief that I can cry for her now because no one did. I am her only voice. I really do love her so much. My heart is filling up with love. Crying makes room for love, and sadness leaves like a shadow when the light is turned on.

Review: What was the effect of writing from these two perspectives?

Example: I feel I have connected another piece of the puzzle. That young girl . . . and her mother. That young girl *was* the mother, and the mother was the child. She starved herself and lost the child. Now the child wants to feed her. Now the daughter is the mother. Mother/daughter. Daughter/mother. Now they have reversed roles. I don't have to be the mother anymore.

As you feel safer about reliving your pain, you will be able to probe deeper. And the deeper you probe, the more fearless you will grow. Remember, part of your safety lies in being able to stop at whatever point you need. You never have to push yourself where you feel unsafe. Whenever you reach such a point, however, acknowledge it in your writing. Then give yourself permission to stop, to ease the pain, and to feel safe.

CHAPTER SEVEN

The Dangers of the Healing Process

*W*hen you feel helpless and hopeless, you are

near to the core of recovery. Allow the pain.

You must break down before you can

break through.

—ALINA PANTERA, teacher

AWARENESS IS LIBERATING. The process of gaining it, however, can be uncomfortable, even painful, and certainly dangerous to the status quo. Discovery of your truths sometimes requires diligent archaeology in treacherous emotional terrain. You may have to see those you love and admire as naked, perhaps even hideous in their faults; you might have to see those you have despised in redemptive light; and you may have to see yourself in ways you have purposefully avoided.

Facing these dangers defeats them. In the light of awareness, our fears diminish, eventually to disappear from the subconscious—and thereby from the conscious mind. With this healing comes the resurgence of energy previously consumed in repression. Sometimes the time and attention needed for this aspect of soul retrieval depends on the depth to which a feeling has been buried or denied. At other times, your readiness will exceed your expectations, and insight is imminent. There is no order of difficulty in consciousness; awareness makes no distinction among degrees or direction of mis-perception. Its self-balancing, self-aligning power is truly indiscrim-inate.

When Terror Strikes

> The only way to succeed in creating is to know that
> it's all right to fail. Risk is the only catalyst for
> innovation. You have to be terrified and use
> that terror to create.
>
> —MANDY PATINKIN, actor

WHEN TERROR STRIKES, the first thing you usually feel is aloneness. The second may be paralysis. The third, if you are writing about your fear, is an overwhelming desire to close your notebook, throw away your pen, walk away from your desk, and do anything at all to distract yourself from your thoughts, your feelings, and this process. If you must disengage, do so. *But do it consciously* by first writing down just how much you don't want to write. Then put your pen down and leave.

Many people bury their hostile, volatile, and disloyal emotions toward those they love or respect with the rationalization that their feelings are unjustified. Justification is irrelevant! The feelings are still unsettling to the emotional and physical body. Some students resist their expression out of the subconscious fear that the expres-sion itself has the power to do harm, as if their words could actually kill.

The more dastardly the act of vengeance we perform on the

page, the healthier the effect. Once during an especially volatile period in my son's adolescence, I was so angry at him that all I could see was a picture of myself dismembering him and boiling him in oil. Of course, the rational, devoted mother in me screamed, "What kind of mother are you! What right do you have to feel such hideous things? He's your own flesh and blood. He's still a child. God knows, he's had his own tribulations!" All the while, my body was responding, "The hell with his tribulations! *My* blood is boiling."

I then reminded myself of what I remind my students: "You are only writing a story. It's like trying on a costume or playing a role. And this story is no more or less real than the one you have been telling yourself." So I wrote the grisliest scene I could imagine:

He has gone too far, and it must stop! Stop NOW! Watch this, you ungrateful little bastard—I'll slice off your arms with my stainless steel sword. Armless, you can't defend yourself from me. And I'll back you into my cauldron, the one already bubbling with boiling oil. I've kept it ready for this moment, scented it with bay leaf so I won't have to smell your rage. Now, at last, *my* torture ends and yours begins.

You sink. The bubbling oil is as deep as your shoulders, and the more you rage, the deeper you sink. I don't care about the anger that shoots from your eyes now. You chose this rage over my love and now you can boil in it.

Go ahead and scream! You've never tolerated pain very well. But don't worry. Soon enough the heat will suck the venom from your muscles. Then you'll have to plead.

Your pleas leave me cold, even as I watch the skin fall away from your bones in raw chunks. Soon you'll be a shrieking skeleton. And then as your bones soften, you'll melt. Your chin will sink into the oil, then your mouth. And then your screams will vanish.

I notice how much your eyes look like mine. Everyone has always told us this. But I've never inhabited your eyes before. Only the rage lived there, and now it is vacating them, fleeing from the very sockets. Look at you, shutting your eyes as your head submerges.

Oil bubbles up around the shadow that is all that is left of you. Then even the bubbling diminishes. The cauldron cools. All that is left of you is the scent of steaming bay leaf.

I felt like the proverbial cackling witch as I wrote. But at least that was a feeling of power. Cackling witches, while not beloved, are certainly perceived as powerful. And while I was, frankly, more horrified at myself for *not* feeling horrified at what I had written, I was relieved at letting go of my wretched impotence. The feeling of power that the writing connected me with simmered me down.

I found myself captivated by the workings of my imagination, and that captivation was deeper than my rancor. Observing my words was like reading a fairy tale—seeing all the dark, menacing, subconscious venom my vulnerable little mother's heart had been harboring spilled across the page. And that was exactly the point— by constructively venting the full extremity of my feelings on the page, I had worked a kind of alchemy and turned inner turmoil into something safe—just as fairy tales provide catharsis for children.

The truth is that regardless of whether we allow ourselves to hear our thoughts and feel our feelings, they persist in the subconscious and in governing our emotions and behavior. Consciousness provides us with choice—to react out of reflex or take action out of deliberation. Taking action before gaining awareness signifies fear or guilt and condemns us to repetition. Without consciousness, we allow ourselves to be run by history—our own, and just as often, our predecessors'.

When Terror Strikes

Assignment: Choose a subject that gives you the "heebie-jeebies." Then, rather than writing about that subject, write about the heebie-jeebies.

Example: Oh God, don't take me, guys! Oh God, don't take me! I think I would die of the tremors (the DT's). It would be like thousands of fingers touching me all at once *from the inside out*—Oh God, Oh God, they'd take me with the fingers puckering my skin from the inside out—like farina when it's cooking. Boiling oatmeal.

They would take me out to the farthest reaches of deepest darkness. Out and out through the deepest water, the burning pools. The nothing, the horror. So close, so fast, like the breath you can't grasp when the roller coaster whooshes you down the slope into power and speed and rushing dark wind. People laugh when that happens, but it's because they're afraid. SO afraid. They flip flop the scream, and it comes out laughter. It's too fast. It's too much. Too much, too much, *too much*. Especially with the fingers poking, kneading, poking, and my organs jumping inside. I can hear it even now as I write, their snickering, chortling like gremlins.

I don't want to go there—to no-man's-land, don't want to be a nowhere man, a cartoon in a cartoon graveyard. It's not the final frontier, it's nothing forever! And my atoms will finally split apart from all the finger poking. I'm upset even now, even as I'm writing this. I don't ever want to think about this place, much less go there. I hate the fucking heebie-jee-bies. They don't give a rat's ass about me!

Review: The next time this student attempted to write about loss and abandonment, his resistance had substantially dim-inished. The subject was still not easy for him to approach, but it was now, at least, accessible. Does your subject feel more or less accessible to you after writing about the creeps it gave you to write about it? Write about how much more or less skittish you feel.

———————

This unearthing of buried feelings and dusting off of skeletal beliefs is dangerous to the ego and can be unsettling for the physical body as well. You may find that you need extra rest and time alone. Take it! Emotional toxicity produces physical toxicity, and you may experience physical symptoms. Pay attention to them. Listen to them. Observe them. Interview them. Drink a lot of water. As an electrical conductor, water promotes movement of energy through your body. It also literally flushes out your system. Have massages to release the effects of negativity imprinted in your muscular system. The more you expel toxins—physical, emotional, or otherwise—the more you contribute to your overall health.

The Value of Crisis

Give thanks to your crises for giving you the power to
not become all that you fear.

—ALINA PANTERA, teacher

INTENSITY IS OFTEN necessary for messages to break through the habitual mental, emotional, or social patterns that have caused dis-ease, disorder, or creative paralysis. Crisis is usually an indicator that previous subtle indications have not been heeded or sufficiently attended. Crisis galvanizes attention, and any action or event that catalyzes a shift in our perspective will open doors to fresh experience and meaning.

A crisis rips apart our accepted, day-to-day plotline, confuses character profiles, and disrupts the scenery of our stories. Although falling in love, making art in any form, and relocation are preferable means of re-viewing or rewriting our stories, crisis can serve as an equally great motivator.

The ego—the part of our personality that projects and insulates our self-image—hates *anything* that disturbs our accepted picture of the world and of the status quo. Crisis typically generates some degree of self-examination, which the ego interprets as a deathly threat. Not only are the circumstances that prompt a crisis unsettling, so is the accompanying affront to the ego.

Writing provides an antidote to the disorientation caused by crisis. It unlatches the psychic gates through which the subconscious voice can speak, connecting us with inner truths. The stories our writing yields allow us to apprehend and derive new meaning from our own experiences. They attune us to our instincts and reinforce self-trust. When viewed as a creative force for transformation, crisis can actually enlarge our power and expand our awareness of ourselves and of the world.

In many cases, our impediments have become our safety net. They may cause pain or make us miserable, but at least they are familiar. They have become part of our identity. We fear we might not know who we would be without them. We might curse the guilt or strictures lain upon us by our religion, but would we *really* be willing to give it up for the sake of our creativity? Or take on a new religion for its sake? Or stay with our religion? Are we willing to give up marriage or a relationship, or to stay with it, or to commit to a partner, if that is what liberation called for? Are we willing to leave a job, or get a job, or stay in a job? Or invest our own money or allow others to support us? Are we truly willing to release our complaints, grudges, vendettas, and vengeance against the world? Are we willing to make sacrifices on behalf of our own creativity? Or, perhaps equally daunting, to *stop* sacrificing?

Through our writing we learn that there is no right or wrong response to any of these questions. There is only self-knowledge. Consider the courage of the student who, after leaving her life of religious orthodoxy, admitted she could never return:

> I can never go back, even though I've wanted to many times. I can't go back to the synagogue we founded, and I can't go back and play make believe and live by communal rule. I can't go back, and I'm in search. In search of who I am. In search of community. In search of respect for things that I hold dear. In search of a sacred place, hallowed ground, a sanctuary within.
>
> And what if I can't find it? Or I find it and someone takes it away? What if I said to myself, "You are a brave, courageous, wonderful, artistic, beautiful, lovable human being who can cook too, and knows how to do laundry." Oh my G-d! They'll try to sell me, and then I'll be a hired slave. They'll call me "wife."
>
> What if I do acknowledge who I am and what I've done? If my siblings or my mother don't take it from me, then the devil will, the evil G-d, the one who causes all the trouble. We wear a red band around our necks and wrists to ward off the angel of death who comes when things are going too well.
>
> Still, I can't go back.

Reevaluating Crisis

Assignment: List the five biggest crises that have occurred in your life. Did you anticipate them or were they unexpected? How closely did they resemble your worst imaginings? What in your life or within yourself changed most after you emerged from them (or from the most dramatic one)?

Example: 1. Leaving home for college—I dreaded it, I lay awake fearing the separation from home *for years* prior. And then the minute I got there, settled in, and watched my parents drive away—I was fine. I was relieved. To my great surprise, I was ok.

2. Telling Chris I wanted a divorce. No, before that was the *realization* that I wanted a divorce, then, telling him was a crisis all its own. It was as difficult, as stomach churning and muscle clenching as I'd imagined. It was like like flailing in a bloody darkness. The horror was in being unable to see how I'd carry on. The mechanism. The path. I felt blinded—and blind-sided. A collision of my own blackest and most dramatic desires. I lost trust in my instincts, lost trust in my vision. Lost my taste for adventure. Like I'd been thrown from a world of living color into one that was dingy, dirty, soiled, ragged, shredded, and torturously unmendable.

3. Adam's breakdown and having him committed. A scenario that wouldn't stop. A scenario that could have killed us both. A scenario in which there were no prescribed avenues, no directions, no answers, no one to say, "Here's what you need to do and here's how to do it." I didn't know if he would survive, I didn't know if I would survive, and I kept thinking that I had to protect Mama and Papa when all along I was the one in almost as much jeopardy as Adam. I prayed, I pleaded with God, I crawled out of bed every day to do whatever I could figure out to do. I wanted to fall apart, I wanted to lie down and dissolve into a thousand melting pieces. But I couldn't because Adam was a violent, broken mess and we were both prisoners of his condition.

4. The second hospital commitment. Getting the court order. Having to watch Adam taken away in handcuffs. I emerged from this crisis determined that it be the last. I realized that the resources for his recovery had been identified, and from now on, it was up to him. I realized that he might not survive, might not choose to use the resources, might

continue headlong down the path to obliteration, but that I didn't have to go with him. Not anymore.

5., 6., 7. And then there was the hurricane, the potentially fatal blood infection when I was 19, in school in Italy, and being molested at nursery school when I was five. It took 45 years to regather that memory and then years more of writing to recognize its impact. Now, with all those threadbare places rewoven, I feel solid again, as alive as the untouched five-year-old was.

Assignment: List five crises you most fear. How much time do you spend anticipating them? What is the likelihood of their occurring?

Example: I fear Mama and Papa's deaths. I fear their suffering long incapacity. I fear Adam falling apart when Papa dies and having another breakdown. I fear becoming incapacitated by depression or injury. I fear financial doom.

I spend far too much time in fear and doubt. None of these things may ever happen, yet every time the phone rings, the thought sprints through my mind that it's news of something happening to Papa. When did I first start worrying like this? Always, always. When have I not! And he's in good health— diminishing perhaps, evaporating into the ethers like an angel ascending. Growing smaller, looking frail, white. Vulnerable to my eyes, but not to theirs. They carry on like . . . troopers. No, not troopers, but happy campers! I'm the one who projects— it's *my* fear of being alone, *my* fear of loss, *my* fear of suffering. I'm projecting like mad. They may well live another decade in good health and die peacefully in their sleep like Papa's mother did. And *I'm* the one who sweats it out. What else is new?

When we are aligned or at-one, when we surrender to a higher power, then divinity, in whatever form we choose to envision it, takes over everything that is not within our conscious control and guides all that is within it. In this way our writing becomes a tool for spiritual growth.

CHAPTER EIGHT

Spiritual Growth and Self-Exploration

The divine grows more conscious as humanity
grows more conscious.

—CARL JUNG

THE SWISS PSYCHIATRIST Carl Jung likened meaninglessness to illness because "it inhibits the fullness of life." He considered neurotic suffering and existential pain to be results of the ego's isolation from archetypal consciousness. "Meaning makes a great many things—perhaps everything—endurable," he wrote.

Jung believed that the individual who has neither a universal nor personal mythology from which to draw meaning becomes addicted to whatever numbs the pain caused by the vacuum of meaning. A simple example would be a workaholic whose meaning in life is drawn not from relationships, creativity, philanthropy, or service but instead from relentless "producing." Without work to fill the void, he or she is left face-to-face with the despair and anxiety of spiritual and/or emotional emptiness.

The release of unhealthy thoughts and behaviors can, despite its ultimately beneficial effect, feel uncomfortable and, at times, even painful. We may find that acknowledging the pain of emptiness can be as frightening as the sickening effects of physical detoxification. Dispelling the illusion of the void requires an environment of great reassurance and safety and one that links us with uplifting archetypes.

Our writing enables us to safely address our fear and our panic over obliterating illusion. The more we write, the more we recognize connections between our thoughts and archetypal imagery and myths. Joseph Campbell described myth as "the public dream" and dream as "the private myth." Understanding of the meaning of universal and personal myths helps to dispel our fear of the void, the infinite empty place we fear lurks inside ourselves and, by projection, in the world at large. Notice in this account written by V. S. Naipaul in the *New Yorker* how one individual's story represents that of his whole community:

> I heard stories like that of the (diplomat) while I walked and drove around Isfahan, while I considered domes and tiles, arches and vaulting, and, at night, the lights of the arcaded bridges over the river. In some unsettling way, a great pain, physical and mental, lay below the old diplomat's civility. Pain was really the subject of his stories; and sometimes a story, though presented as the experience of someone he knew, had a quality of folk myth, something fabricated out of the general need, just as, at certain times in communities jokes appear and make the rounds, made up by no one but contributed to by everyone.

At the deepest levels of consciousness, visionary work propels our beliefs into a larger, timeless dimension—one that honors archetypal power. Fairy tales, myths, and stories from all history grow meaningful. Their instruction reassures us that the path of inner guidance leads to healing. We find personal meaning in everything from the *Odyssey* to the Song of Solomon to the tale of Little Red Riding Hood. We understand how Orpheus's descent into Hades represents our conscious descent into our own inner turmoil, how the parting of the Red Sea symbolizes our own path from the slavery of doubt to spiritual liberation, how the proverbial wolf at the door is the face of our own fear. Through stories, we are tutored about the ways of sex, love, money, relationships, birth, death, and transformation. Through archetypes, we are shown the way. Through visionary work, we gain full access to our own as well as the universal past and future.

The more we write, the more we recognize how the truths we seek are evident everywhere, in every circumstance, whether negative or positive. This expanding insight brings us wisdom—and greater faith.

Distinguishing Between Faith and Hope

FAITH DERIVES FROM inner knowledge, from an internal connection to a higher source. Hope, on the other hand, derives from belief that the power that shapes our lives is external. Liberation from doubt and fear requires surrender to a greater power. Hope can stall release and delay surrender. Faith welcomes surrender. Faith, more than hope, opens the door to liberation and eases our passage. Your writing provides a means of exercising faith.

I like to think of faith as a muscle, a part of the spiritual anatomy that, to be healthy, requires the same kind of attention as the physical anatomy. Without exercise, the muscles grow weak. Without spiritual exercise, we allow inspired thoughts, feelings, attitudes, and behaviors to be consumed by negativity. It is irrelevant whether the negativity is subtle or blatant, because the subconscious mind is purely literal in its receptivity to thought. A growing consciousness requires the constant nourishment of enlightened thoughts, images, and sensations as well as the consistent exercise of faith.

This writing process uses the power of incantation to promote inspiration. It draws from your imagination into your conscious mind images that create a sense of possibility, of attaining that which lies beyond your control. This broadened vision opens you to the intervention of that mysterious healing force known, by one name or another, as grace. The more we exercise faith, the greater is our experience of grace. Here is a piece of writing from my own pages:

> I don't know where the strength came from time after time after time. But of course I do. From their vision. From my vision. I thought it was simply ambition. Or pride. Or even shame. Keep going, no matter what. Don't lose face.
>
> But my face was a wreck. My nervous system was a wreck. My compass was skewed from the moment of impact. And yet, I made it, Jona made it, Mother and Daddy made it. We all made it. Back to each other and to our individual gladness. Each of us glad in our own way. And despite the decades of sickness and health, richness and poverty, despite the skewed compasses and searing laments and violent railings at each other and at that vacuum I considered God to be—an unhearing God, the God-of-Never-Listening, of Never-Listening-to-Me—despite it all, I veered to the light. And the light brought me home. And made me at home in my own home. At last.

Grace, like stories, asks only to be received. Like stories, it does not require that we do, be, or act. Grace, like stories, asks only that we listen. Art and healing occur when we respond to the incantatory summoning of grace. Our stories beckon us.

Judgment—An Opening
to the Labyrinth

OUR WRITING ALLOWS us to use judgment as a siren, a spotlight, a stale or putrid odor that can lead us to purification. We do not attempt to erase judgment or even to resist it—because what we resist persists. Instead, by observing our judgments, we realize how much energy they cost.

We liberate the energy to create a new experience of our own reality by observing how we organize our lives around a belief. If, for example, we believe the world is divided—between blacks and whites, women and men, Jews and gentiles, fat and slender, rich and poor, educated and uneducated—we fail to see universal qualities in everything, everywhere. As we observe our own policies of segregation, we begin to recognize where we are excluding our own possibility.

Spiritually, to sin, or "miss the mark," is to think judgmentally, unforgivingly, or with thoughts that separate us from others. Here are one student's thoughts about sin:

Something in me recoils at my sins, which are legion. I am always guilty of something. I am never innocent, especially when I proclaim loudly that someone has hurt me, has emotionally raped me, has denigrated me. There is always the sin, the shame lurking below the abuse, the challenge, the heavy slights up and down my body. They are legion.

They are not accidents. They are my destiny. To be sinned against, to be sinning, to be wrong, to be guilty, to be ashamed, to be blamed. It is always my fault. I am always at risk—of shame, of sticking out—so as to tear this shame out of my body. I need to fling it out. If someone shames me, abuses me, or defends me, or shows me to be looking bad, incompetent, anything, it is the mark of shame coming out like the scarlet letter.

The word *repentance* is derived from the French word *repenser,* meaning "to think again." We can interpret sin as thought that is unaligned with truth, and repentance as thought realigned. Therefore, true atonement (or *at-one-ment*) for conceptually missing the mark is to think again—without thoughts of separation and with a view toward wholeness, toward fulfillment, toward filling spiritual holes or psychic wounds. Atonement is to think in alignment with divine thought.

Consider the example of a student who felt she was being emotionally devoured by her fiancé and wanted to break off the engagement. First, I asked her to write about being devoured.

I am something you eat—something to be absorbed into another's system, chemically changed in another's body in order to perpetuate life, give pleasure, provide adornment. You can devour me when you understand how to get the milk out of me—like out of a coconut. You can throw me against the side of a tree, take a hammer to me or smash me against the sidewalk.

You can open me up real wide, but you will never have me. It's true, you can get the meat, but not the sweet, sweet milk that is left on the side of the tree, dripping from the hammer or splattered all over the sidewalk.

I ask you, "What is it you want?" "The milk," you say. At first glance you might think there is this hard shell, two at that. They make it difficult to get at what's inside. You roll me in your hands, searching, touching, and yearning for the sweet meat and the heaven-made milk. "But how do I get inside?" you ask.

To get my milk you would have to stop before you throw me against the tree, before you take up a hammer or smash me against the sidewalk. Take me in your hand, touch me, feel me and understand me . . . and I will give you my milk.

This student's anger, her desire to "be right and *win*" over her lover was causing the "sin" or misalignment of her thinking. I asked her to think of her fiancé as a mirror of her own anger and to write about how *she* wanted to devour *him*. "Oh no, I couldn't even *imagine* that," she answered. "Then turn your writing around," I suggested, "and substitute 'I' for 'you.'" The "repentance" sounded like this:

> You are something I eat. I devour you when I understand how to get the milk out of you—like out of a coconut. I throw you against the side of a tree, take a hammer to you and smash you against the sidewalk.
>
> You ask me, what is it I want? The milk, I say. I roll you in my hands, searching, touching, and yearning for your sweet meat and heaven-made milk. But how do I get inside you? I ask.
>
> To get your milk I would have to stop before I throw you against the tree, before I take up the hammer and smash you against the sidewalk. Take you in my hand, touch you, feel you, and understand you—and you will give me your milk.

The "repentant" image so resonated for this student that she was able to recognize the destructive power of her own deep judgment. She could then relent in her mission to "fix" her fiancé and concentrate on ameliorating her own anger. *This* was the healing, *not* the subsequent restoration of or extrication from the relationship.

The stronger you connect with your innate inner knowledge, the more you become able to surrender the impulse to change, fix, or conquer. Your mission in this process is to develop understanding and create meaning rather than engineer a particular outcome. Your writing is not intended to discover a "cure" or remove a problem but rather to find the nourishment or enlightenment the problem offers. It is *not* a tool for righting a wrong, for that belief implies guilt or self-blame, and healing occurs with the surrender of blame. Blame produces toxicity and is as poisonous as self-flagellation, self-mutilation, and self-denial, which are *not* reasonable means of atonement—or healing. By writing you weave together the threads of your stories, providing you with the wholeness to create new, forgiving ones.

Forgiveness Promotes Miraculous Vision

Miracles are everyone's right, but purification is necessary first.

—FOUNDATION FOR INNER PEACE, *A Course in Miracles*

Our spirit is very much a part of our daily lives; it embodies our thoughts and emotions, and it records every one of them, from the most mundane to the visionary. . . . Every second of our lives . . . is somehow known and recorded. Every judgment we make is noted. Every attitude we hold is a source of positive or negative power for which we are accountable.

—CAROLINE MYSS, PH.D., *Anatomy of the Spirit*

THE WRITING PROCESS taught in this book is more than a journal of events or recording of ideas. It can provide what the religious confessional offers the true supplicant—a place to bare your soul, relieve your mind, and empty your heart. It is a process by which you gain inner absolution. It is the true "account" of your experiences, emotions, thoughts, dreams, fears, and hopes.

The ultimate goal of both healing and high art is to replace unforgiving vision with miraculous vision. An unforgiving vision is one frozen in time and perspective; a miraculous vision flows with nourishing possibilities.

Forgiveness frees us from judgment—from viewing the world with thoughts of punishment and attack. It removes fear, guilt, pain, all sense of weakness, strain, and fatigue from the mind. It also promotes the flow of energy around a thought that previously had been fixed in judgment. New sensations occur with this restored circulation along with shifts in perception.

Our writing brings us to the discovery—or rediscovery—that forgiveness is the most effective tool in transforming destructive pain into creative power. I speak of forgiveness here not as approval but instead as a willingness to see from another point of view. To forgive is to revise a thought colored with judgment (of any kind and to any degree) into a thought free of judgment. To forgive is to think again (repent) without judgment.

When you heal through forgiveness, you surrender blame—even toward the illness itself. Even if the physical pain continues, forgiveness frees you from the emotional anguish—the suffering— caused by feelings of guilt or thoughts of blame. It soothes your body, heals your heart, and metaphysically nourishes all life. Forgiveness restores your awareness of your divine invulnerability, and it extends grace, simultaneously toward yourself and others.

The conscious mind alone, however, cannot enact forgiveness, no matter how determined you are. The subconscious mind must also be willing to let go of attack thoughts, and if it harbors any degree of guilt, shame, or anger, then forgiveness remains incomplete. You cannot forgive completely until you have acknowledged the depth of the wound.

Through your writing, you can vent your anguish safely, expressing it as loudly and desperately as possible. You can sob, moan, wail, berate, dismember, disembowel, ignite, and annihiliate to your heart's content. You can allow a feeling to take as long as necessary to be released. More often than not, that length of time is a surprise. Healing has its own timetable.

Miraculous vision emanates not from the darkness of despair but from the light of consciousness. Your ability to visualize surges when you free unforgiving thoughts from the subconscious by acknowledging them. This shifts your perceptions, stimulating insight and creativity. Any perceptual shift is miraculous when it diminishes judgment, perpetuates forgiveness, or expands awareness. Miraculous vision extracts wholeness from fragmentation leading us to see how, as *A Course in Miracles* teaches, "We are a miracle, capable of creating in the likeness of our Creator. Everything else is our own nightmare, and does not exist. Only the creations of light are real."

Do not be concerned if this thinking seems strange, unapproachable, or even radical. The purpose of this work is to bring nearer the time when these ideas will feel wholly natural. The process leads indisputably to self-knowledge, and self-knowledge brings pleasure and peace of mind, and they, in turn, bring emotional and physical healing.

In the following example, notice how the student's typical defensiveness toward her sister is transformed to wonder and compassion through the nonjudgmental act of observation:

> Just the day before, I'd broken from a mid-morning walk on the beach to knock on Randi's motel room door. She, making grouper salad, surprised in her domesticity, was unencumbered by the layers of purposefulness she usually bears—the makeup, hair, arrangement of outlandish clothing and clunky costume jewelry. I was surprised to see how young she was, the few faint freckles; have they always been there and I never knew? Even as I acknowledged the subterfuge implied by all this, I warmed to her; she seemed so . . . innocent.
>
> I wanted to bring her back to the house with me, unfettered, in this pristine state, and let Andrew see . . . see what? He wouldn't be seeing what I can't help but see, the little girl she once was whose pudgy arm stretched high to meet my grasp, her hand almost too tiny to close around my thumb. No, she was long gone even those many years ago.

And what if Andrew had first met her here, now, scrubbed like this: before the silver baseball cap and matching silver sandals, before the anchorwoman makeup (at the beach, *Jesus*)! Would he have seen her differently? If he had withheld his gift of relief and bade me accept my lot, my karma, my family, would I then have to mire myself in their sweaty intrigues; be with them, in their darkness, like bait-worms writhing in the soft mud at the edge of the lake; just under surface, slithering over each other's bodies, going nowhere, waiting, to be scooped up or rot?

The greatest challenge you will confront in this process is allowing yourself to lose your reputation with *yourself*. The more you write, the more benign, ludicrous, and informative a mirror the world becomes. As a consequence, your resistance to facing your ego will diminish.

Facing the Ego

> Giocometti's drawings and paintings show his
> bewilderment and persistence. If he had not
> acknowledged his bewilderment, he would
> not have persisted.

> —ANNIE DILLARD

"So WHAT IF I'm not plagued by unsettling emotion or significant 'blocks'?" some might ask. "What if annoyance is the worst that afflicts me?"

"Then you are making your ego quite happy," would be my answer. Like science, the literal mind believes that things are only as they appear. As I stated earlier, scientific, logical, or linear thinking is based on the objective weighing of fact and detail and calls on a mode of "seeing without imagination." Myth—nonliteral, nonlogical, and imbued with imaginary color, texture, and detail—cannot be fully understood without entering into a metaphysical state of mind. Transformation requires a merging or dissolution into a larger, more encompassing identity than that of the ego.

To grow, you must risk learning that you are not who you thought you were and not who you have told the world you are. Even worse, you may realize that you're exactly what you have most feared or resisted ("Oh my God! I *am* my mother!").

When you write, you turn the tables on the fragile ego, which prefers that you ignore or try to eradicate unpleasant, unacceptable, or painful feelings. Instead, you make those feelings louder, more visible, more clawing, claustrophic, and repulsive, more frivolous, banal, and ridiculous, more ambitious, animated, and exultant. The very extremity of your expression blasts your feelings to the fore and gives you the opportunity to consciously determine your willingness to preserve or revise them.

As Alina Pantera explains, "The freedom to be conscious of your negative emotions and *not* act on them leads to a full emotional life, a fully present life, a healed and healthy life. You cannot be scared, angry, bored or sad when you are living totally in the present. You are healed when you no longer hate or distrust what you feel." Here is how one student gingerly approached her long-resisted feelings of anger.

> Anger really makes me sick. Especially with strangers. You have to control it, but it controls you. Air gets sucked out of my body. I dry up like a shellfish on the shore, shriveled and shrunken under the sun of anger.
>
> But this is the sun of my life. As much as I fear the emotion, anger is also my way to detoxify myself. I can't live without it! I go up and down the elevator of my anger. Up to my heart and lungs where it burns. The place where tobacco used to nest in my body. The tobacco road of anger.
>
> Cigarette smoking was an addiction. Up and up to the throat.

I can't speak the unspeakable. I usually cry when I try. I cry this inappropriate self out of my body. Out of my lungs, my liver, my skin.

Anger is water. It's a pump. A fluid. I will drown in my own tears.

Give me a hug and I will take the trip down the elevator. Go back to the irritated muscles, the disassembled pieces of my anatomy down to my guts where a serene fire awaits. A hug and my tears would dry as well. I shall speak then.

What is the taste of our delicious anger? Can I perfume my life with it? Can we share our anger? Can we bathe in the same sacramental bathtub?

I've been fed with my parents' anger. They have nurtured me with it. In order to be free, I must be loveless. For love is the most beautiful wrapping of the gift of anger; it is the magnificent bullshit we all live by. We cry for love. We starve for love. But, finally, what's the difference between love and the food rotting now in my stomach.

Secrets breed deceit. When we keep our feelings in the dark, we deceive ourselves. We also deprive ourselves of the power we are using to keep our feelings hidden. Therefore, we must look not only at our fears but also at the illusion of safety we believe the darkness provides.

Under Cover

Assignment: Complete a sentence that begins "I only feel safe under cover . . . " and keep writing.

Example: I only feel safe under cover . . . of the secular world. How can I tell my story to my people and family when I am afraid I would be punished, forget not being understood.

My fear of banishment is very real—undercover—I've led my entire life undercover until now. And I'm tired of having to hide anymore.

I hate the secrets that were forced on me. I wasn't allowed to tell my friends about my mentally ill father or talk about my mother's beatings. I was always afraid I would be punished more. I couldn't tell my husband about having a convulsion 3 weeks before my wedding. "How could you do this to me?" was Mother's cry. "How could you leave me with the burden of marrying you off as a convulsive daughter of a mentally ill father. Remember, you are a Bas Moshe, and don't you forget it, but don't let anybody else know. Cover it up. Be clean and smart and talented and don't tell your family's secrets in public or anywhere else."

"Don't expose your dirty laundry, emotional pornography," my brother said of my article where I discussed my father's illness. And my Chassidic rabbi ex-husband surfs the net undercover as a lesbian!!!

Example: I only feel safe under cover. Cover? Cover what? I need a cover? You bet I do! How can I live without my two selves? I need to be the moon, and I need my solar energy. I need to be a woman and a man. I need the light and the dark. I need to be Annabelle and Vera Hills. I'm not the moon. People wouldn't understand my disappearance into darkness or my need to reflect. People wouldn't let me breathe. In and out. Inward and outward. Annabelle, Anna, Vera, Eva, Land, Hills. Who else? A cover is the air we breathe.

Review: How much of your time and energy goes into maintaining the images you believe others have of you? How close does your image of yourself come to one you try to project? Write about this proximity or distance.

Assignment: Your cover is blown! Your daily pages have been discovered by the person(s) you most feared seeing them. Write about it.

Example: My family has just found my journal. I don't want to write about it. I might die. Found out. Such a temper, such anger. Who is this person? Not our child, sister, mother. OK, my daughter would believe it. She's known me all her life, and I don't think you can hide things from your own children. They just know.

But the exaggerations are frightening. I mean I could probably write horror stories, but nothing that actually makes sense. Or babbling along with fuzzy images and then just reaching up and plucking some gem of wisdom. I'd have to explain that they were plucked from my heart. Blame Laura.

Review: How do you feel now that you've been exposed? Where in your body do you most feel it?

———————

In most spiritual practices, the term *truth* refers to thinking that is aligned with the Divine. Through this alignment, we are connected with the pure energy that manifests life and its innate joy. The pure experience of that pure energy is what we know as *love*. You will find as your writing brings about alignment . . . and love, that healing is its own reward.

PART THREE

Art, Passion, and Creativity

Art is meant to be disturbing, to ask questions. It's not meant to take us out of ourselves. It's meant to put us more into ourselves.

—EDWARD ALBEE, playwright

Real passion occurs only when there is a giving up of oneself, an abandonment. Only in passion is there a quality of attention fundamental to learning.

—JOEL KRAMER, author

The generation of ideas involves factors that are not exclusively cerebral, factors that include the physiology, the emotions, and the outer world.

—ROBERT GRUDIN, *The Grace of Great Things*

CHAPTER NINE

Our Power Lives in Our Stories

*S*tories set the inner life into motion.

—CLARISSA PINKOLA ESTES,

Women Who Run with the Wolves

*S*o much of living is made up of storytelling that one might conclude that it is what we were meant to do—to tell one another stories, fact or fiction, as a way of keeping afloat. Job's messenger, Coleridge's mariner, the reporter on the Rancho Santa Fe cult all grab us by the lapels to tell us their tale. We do the same; we cannot help ourselves. We have the story of others to tell, or of ourselves, or of the species— some monumentally elusive tale we are always trying to get right. Sometimes it seems that we are telling one another parts of the same immense story. Fiction and [fact] are joined in an endless chain. *Everything is news, everything imagined.*

—ROGER ROSENBLATT, *The New York Times*

The Power of
Incantation

Never be afraid to kill off your characters.

—BRENDAN GILL, author, critic, mentor

THROUGH INCANTATION—THE power of storytelling—we lift the spell of the old stories that have outlived their purpose, and we cast the spell of new creation from which we draw meaning and nourishment.

Dis-ease occurs when we forget that we are the writer—the director of the plot, the author of the words. Once we are unencumbered by the habits of judgment and striving, we create freely. The flow of thoughts and ideas relieves the conscious mind from comparison, analysis, resentment, and guilt—and from the ego. As we create, we grow free to use any vocabulary, voice, or character. Released from struggle, we regain ease.

Creativity begins at any point in time or place. We can start from the outside of a story or picture and work in, or from the inside and work out. In my own artwork, I often begin with the frame and work toward the inside; I start with the architecture or form of the piece and get to the "subject" through a process of playing with materials and composition. I allow them to *lead me* to the focus, to something that will inevitably carry a deep conscious or unconscious meaning whose significance I reevaluate from its "reframing."

Creativity frees us from learned notions of "precious" and "worthless." As we create, we move beyond the subjective values we have attached to certain subjects, objects, or materials and allow ourselves to "play recklessly" through our creations. As we recognize the infinite supply of ideas and materials available to us, we gain security. Everything is grist for the mill, ripe for the picking, and even subject to elimination. As Annie Dillard offers, "The impulse to save something good for a better place later is the signal to spend it now. . . . Similarly, the impulse to keep to yourself what you have learned is not only shameful, it is destructive. Anything you do not give freely and abundantly becomes lost to you."

Writing provides a venue in which we can play God and really witness our willingness to claim our power. The work of the artist Christo is a dramatic example of this point. His monumental wrap projects require years of planning, millions of dollars in financing, the labor of hundreds to assemble. Yet his projects are as intentionally ephemeral as they are massive in scale. They appear over a short span of time—whole buildings or geographic sites visibly altered—and within days or weeks completely disappear.

Pure creativity requires a willingness to destroy the creation, to let it go, to surrender it to its own fate. Like a child we have conceived and borne, our writing—our art—must ultimately be allowed a life of its own.

The Artist As Healer

There was nothing to do but wait,
remember, write. . . .

—ISABEL ALLENDE, *Paula*

AN ARTIST IS one who uses limitation as a means of expansion and expansion as a means to focus. An artist is one who sees chaos as material for gaining clarity and suffering as substance for enlightenment. An artist is more concerned with finding his or her personal truth than being considered "right" or accepted. An artist is one who is willing to let go of *anything* that stands in the way of his or her new creation.

In this way art and healing are synonymous: Both ask us how much change we are willing to allow in order to create wholeness, how much we are truly willing to risk for the sake of our new creation, regardless of whether that creation is a healthy body, a peaceful mind, a different career, a new relationship, or the great universal novel. Are we willing to risk our reputations—with our family, with our friends, with our colleagues or associates, with the world at large, and, hardest of all, with ourselves? Are we willing to sacrifice cherished memories and lifelong beliefs? Are we willing to be "wrong?" Are we willing to surrender? Are we willing to give up our pain?

When we write using the process taught in this book, we learn how to allow old stories to die and be put to rest. We give them their conscious telling, thank them for their service, and, ultimately, send them on their way. We make room for a new generation of stories whose content and telling bring healing and life.

As both healer and artist, it is vital to heed the vulnerability of your newborn creation and protect it from physical, emotional, or physical negativity. Give your writing your labor, and it delivers you. Practice it devoutly. Share it discreetly.

When tenderly fostered and diligently cultivated, our creativity flowers—and must be celebrated. What we acknowledge increases. Increased creativity generates increased health.

Lifting the Spell

We cause the dark side of creation to become struck
with light when we rout our personal demons out
into the light of day.

—CARL JUNG

FOR OUR STORIES to become the substance of art and a vehicle for healing, we must "lie with them," finding all their matching parts inside ourselves. We will see that as the story grows, our consciousness grows and healing occurs. The more precisely we recognize the derivation of our thoughts, the more power we engage. We are, in fact, *stalking* the energy. By throwing a spotlight on our judgments, fears, and discomforts, we can recognize their source within us. This aligns us, and illusion dissolves.

In other words, when your buttons get pushed, decorate them! Wrap them in bows, paint them in neon, stud them with nails, drape them in pearls. Do whatever it takes to identify those buttons as yours. Demonstrate to yourself that they belong to you and not those whose push them. Then alchemy occurs. Transformation results. You have created art. You are healing.

Common "spells" are stories promulgated by society and swallowed whole by the culture. For example, the one I encounter most often among women is that growing old portends loneliness and destitution. I asked a happily married and highly successful professional woman who was nearing retirement age to write on her impending old age. Even with the great fiscal and emotional securities of her life, she wrote:

> I'll be alone, destitute . . . and frenetic, just as I suspected I
> would be. Especially because I thought that doing so much for
> so many others would bring me a free ride at some point in my
> life. But no, most of the people I sacrificed for are dead. Those
> who aren't have forgotten me since I can't do much for them
> anymore. So did I support so many people because I wanted to?
> Was it a sense of duty? Or did I think there was a pay back here
> on earth?
>
> At any rate, I'm alone. It has made me so frightened that I'm
> afraid to sleep. So I keep my self up (much as I did before) to
> write my memoirs—if there's anyone left to read them. I also

watch TV incessantly, like I always wanted to do. But the real reason is that I'm afraid to sleep for fear it will be the last time I close my eyes. Actually being alone is not much different from having surrounded myself with people.

I asked this student to pursue the fear and to write about the *real* fear—mortality, the ultimate aloneness, the final destitution, the eternal sleep. She responded:

Death is the only pass to freedom. . . . Bullshit! That's the depression I have been fighting always. Who said, "Life is sitting in a row boat in the middle of a lake with no oars." Well, I reject that existential nonsense, too. If you don't have oars, use your arms!

Surely I can unshackle myself from this notion that I cannot free myself without dying. What kind of freedom do I mean? Attachment? Anchors? What?

I can free myself. I know that because I freed myself from the ultimate fear of death—my father's rage and my mother's terror. I've decided to un-existential myself.

The following exercises give you an opportunity to identify various spells you are under and their sorcerers. Who cast them, what service did or do they provide, and do you wish to remain under them?

Under the Spell

Assignment: Complete a sentence that begins "I am under the spell of . . . " and keep writing.

Example: I am under the spell of the youth-worshiping advertising culture that makes me feel like I'm growing old exponentially fast, that makes me see the grey hairs growing in my 28-year-old head as more than just troublesome, not simply something to be plucked before they become too obvious.

Soon my entire head will be grey, and my hair will grow all the way down my back, and I'll keep it in a big bun at the nape of my neck. I'll sell beaded necklaces off a cart and wear tie-dyed wrinkly skirts and stop shaving my legs so I'll look like an old hippie grandma. But I'll love my grey hair, my long grey beautiful hair. I'll remember how it used to be pretty and golden in the sunlight. But I'll like it even more when I'm old, because I'll be liking it strictly because it's mine.

Everyone will say, "You should cut that hair or dye it." And I'll smile, knowing I don't have to please anyone, that I can find myself beautiful all by myself.

And the faint wrinkles that now disappear with a healthy diet and plenty of rest, they will become deeply engraved, revealing my past like the lines on my palm reveal my future. It will show all the care and worries and hopes and dreams and excitements and upsets. The whole story of my life will be carved into my face. I am such a child to all the lives and lessons ahead of me.

Assignment: Complete a sentence that begins "I am under my own spell about . . . " and keep writing.

Example: I am under my own spell about how I will live out my old age *totally* alone. Without even plants or weeds. No dogs or cats. No cats or friends, family, child. No publishers, accountants, bookkeepers, travel agents, gardeners, electricians, car mechanics, drywall installers, tenants, ditch diggers, telephone repairmen, utility guys, garbage men, waitresses, short-order cooks, fellow travelers of any sort. Nothing. No one. Nowhere.

Well, at least there could be beautiful furniture. Endless rooms of objets d'art and canvas and stone and pigment and echo. Echoing halls. Hair painted into canvas. A reminder of someone, some being who once was part of my life and never will be again. This is not hermetic—or is it? This is not air-less—or is it?

Not even a cycad, alive and growing to oxygenate the air I breathe and to tantalize me with its scent! No flowers. No grass. No fragrance. Can I live a life without fragrance? Without taste? Without touch? That, of course, would be the hardest. No touch. No warm hands or fingers or lips. No caress. No one to brush aside a fallen lock of hair or errant tear. No screams or pliant cries to hear or respond to. As a matter of fact, there would be nothing to respond to except the echoes of my own mind. A resonant madness. A mad resonance.

———————

You dispel the power of an old story by relentlessly observing each and all of its many facets. By turning the story from side to side and upside down, telling it from the outside in and the inside out, inflating it and deflating it. You cannot cast a new spell, until you recognize the present one.

Casting a Spell

Go out and let stories happen to you, work with
them, water them with your blood and tears and your
laughter till they bloom, till you yourself burst into
bloom. Then you will see what medicines they make,
and where and when to apply them.
This is the work. The only work.

—CLARISSA PINKOLA ESTES,
Women Who Run with the Wolves

WE CAST A spell through visionary seeing. We revise our stories through our imaginations. The new spells we cast, which are nourished by past experience, present power, and future ideas, reanimate our lives.

Free from the paralysis of fear, doubt, anger, resentment, regret, or vengeance, we dance. We have the power to change our roles from large to small or small to large. We grow from fearful to fearless when we realize that regimentation freezes the frame in the movies of our lives and that flexibility advances the action. We see how, as one of my students wrote, "Poetry begins where the drama ends." By freeing ourselves from our old stories, we transcend cultural conditioning and gain the courage to claim our personal freedom.

This writing process will initiate you into the practice of alchemy—the transformation of unseen forces that turns the shadow into light. This alchemical power is ignited by our willingness to suspend disbelief. The writer and film director Laura Esquivel, creator of *Like Water for Chocolate,* lovingly talks about the willingness of her audience or reader to accept the fantastical: "That tears shed into the batter of a wedding cake could make all the guests at the ceremony wail for their own lost loves; granting that rose petals used to perfume a quail sauce could send a señorita scampering naked as a dog in heat across the Mexican horizon to find her true love and become a general in a revolution."

Our imaginations grow as we step deeper into the world of the visionary. We find ourselves increasingly more receptive to possibilities that lie beyond our control. This openness, a mysterious healing force, is known by one name or another as grace. One student described the experiences of grace in her writing: "When I get outside of my thoughts enough to see them on the page, I have moments of insight that I can only call *grace*. I do not understand this any more than I understand any other act of creation. I only know that I emerge out of my 'stuckness' with a sense of movement and of gratitude for my life."

Grace is a free-flowing effect of awareness just as awareness is a free-flowing effect of grace. Comparison, analysis, doubt, and resentment inhibit awareness and, therefore, the ability to receive grace.

CHAPTER TEN

Creative Release and Overcoming Blocks

I now see, hear, and smell the sawdust, the almost circus-like atmosphere of art in my brain.

—MONIKA BURG, writing student

THE MORE WE practice this writing process, the keener our instincts grow and the safer we feel about our own choices. One student described it this way: "My brain was so clogged that I no longer trusted my ability to make even the most basic decisions. But now the patterns are so clear and logical that, for the first time, maybe ever, I have peace of mind. I don't have all the answers, but I no longer fear the questions."

Progressive emotional release triggers corresponding physical response and shifts in habits, attitudes and will. "Blocks" disappear. Creativity beckons. As the writer Robert Grudin has put it, "Original thought is the product not of the brain, but of the full self."

Creativity promotes challenge, resistance, and unsettledness. It is not surprising, then, that creativity is regarded as treacherous to authoritarian bodies, totalitarian governments, and adherents to the status quo. In *The Grace of Great Things*, Robert Grudin writes, "We cannot open ourselves to new insight without endangering the security of our prior assumptions. We cannot propose new ideas without risking disapproval and rejection. Creative achievement is the boldest initiative of mind, an adventure that takes (us) simultaneously to the rim of knowledge and the limits of propriety."

In the following example, one student tracked her recollection of an adolescent initiation whose meaning had lingered, poignant and unarticulated, until the writing:

I was in no way attracted to Rick . . . he was acne-faced and had no personality. But I was counting on him to show me what a kiss felt like. I was fourteen, in ninth grade, and had never had someone else's lips on mine.

Rick had called and asked if I would meet him on the golf course (which was right behind my house). My friend Annie had told me that when a guy wanted to have sex with her, she would just pretend to have her period. That was my plan too. (The thought that Annie might actually have *agreed* to have sex had not occurred to me.)

Rick showed up at my bedroom window, and I crawled out. We started walking across the golf course, I in my pajamas and he in jeans and a T-shirt. As he walked (on my right), his left hand slid around my neck and over to my left breast. This was the first time a boy had ever touched my breast.

"Hmmmm . . . they're a lot bigger than I thought! What size are they?" he said.

"C," I answered, grateful for the compliment and trying to sound cheery. Actually I was starting to feel a little queasy.

We hadn't been walking for very long and were only a short distance from my neighbors' backyards when he sat us down. I was expecting my kiss. I had been expecting it ever since his arm went around my neck, but once again it seemed that I was going to play "second" to my ample chest.

He lifted up my pajama top, and his mouth went immediately to my beasts. He was kissing *them* just as I had imagined would happen on my mouth! I thought, "This is an unusual place to start." I figured the kiss would eventually rise northward to satisfy my curiosity. Then I would have a kiss to run through my imagination and play back whenever needed.

The licks turned into sucks, and I could feel Rick's penis (did he open his jeans?) hard against my leg. Now I was feeling *more* putrid. Finally, Rick looked up and asked if I gave Ben blow jobs. Ben was a guy in school who I had the maddest raving crush on. Hearing about Ben and his girlfriend made my hair absolutely stand on end. And now, here was Rick assuming I was Ben's girl-friend. It seemed like quite a compliment. But what was this business about blow jobs?

I told him no, I didn't give Ben blow jobs. Then he asked if I would give *him* a blow job. Again I answered no.

Taking his hands away from my breasts, Rick pulled my pajama top back down and stood up. His jeans were around his ankles, but he still had his boxers on. He pulled up his pants while I got to my feet. Then he walked me part of the way home and said goodbye. No kiss.

I crawled through my bedroom window and tiptoed into the bathroom. As I sat down to pee, I looked at the bath mat. It was littered with grass that had stuck to my feet. I thought about how dirty my feet were, how dirty the mat was, and how dirty the carpet in my room must be. I felt like a little part of me was dirty too. It was like when my parents got divorced or when my front teeth broke. It was permanent. That was what all those creepy things had in common. None could be fixed once the perfection was broken.

Healing occurs with the restoration of balance. Art occurs at the edge—of the known, the safe, the expected. Both require unrelenting observation and detachment. The more creative we grow, the more vital is our need for balance.

Dynamic Balance

Communication never occurs when there's either
dominance or submission. The very nature of
dominance and submission destroys the energy
of communication.

—JOEL KRAMER

EXPRESSION IS VITAL to growth, wholeness, and healing. Passionate expression can transform experience into art, no matter how long forgotten, deeply buried, or seemingly unacceptable. The healing power of creativity derives from a dynamic balance between passion and detachment and between introspection and expression.

Passion generates healing energy; detachment, in providing distance from habitual thoughts and feelings, creates an opening through which this passion-generated energy can surge. Detachment also enables us to fearlessly identify and focus on the flaw, fear, or judgment that is generating toxicity in the body and the mind.

Through this writing process, we safely descend into the darkness of the subconscious where our fears and vengeance hide. There we become emotional alchemists, stirring up our psyches, later to transmute our pain into power.

Art, like alchemy, occurs at the point of the most exquisite tension. This was made palpable to me recently at an exhibition of a friend's minimalist artwork. Minimalism reduces the formal qualities of line, color, shape, and surface texture to essentials, without concern for realistic detail, illusionistic space, or storytelling. With my preference for narration and for baroque creations, not surprisingly, I am not a fan of this style. However, despite my prejudice, I approached the exhibit pleased on behalf of my friend and curious about what I would see (though I was still half expecting to be bored by yet another series of flat color fields and monotonous shaped canvases). But as soon as I entered the gallery, my eyes fell across a taut, nearly monochromatic canvas across the center of which two fine wires had been tightly strung. The juxtaposition of the taut wires against the exquisite subtlety of the monotone magnetized my attention—and for the first time in my art career, I recognized beauty in a minimalist work. The contrast between the "calm" of the surface and the contained turbulence of the wire tension created a psychological—and probably optical—shift in my vision. Without that degree of tension, the piece could not have generated its power.

The sanctuary that writing daily provides pulls taut the boundaries around your creativity—and health—and allows you to work safely on the edge. The process enables you to "try your boundaries on for size" to see when, where, and how you feel safest. Knowing this, you then can ask yourself how closely you *are willing* to draw those boundaries—in terms of time, activity, space, and, of course, identity. Are you willing to give up meditation, sleep, reading, creative activities, or studio space to accommodate your parents, friends, children, or employers? Sometimes yes, sometimes no, sometimes never? How far will you go to protect your creativity? How committed are you to your own health, to your peace of mind?

Obstacles to My Creativity

Assignment: List the five things you most need in order to concentrate on your creative activities (such as time to draw or read, a place to work, money for materials). List those people who create obstacles to your having these. How much time and energy do you give each person on this list? What is the greatest danger—for you or them—that would be presented by your having unrestrained access to your creativity?

Example: Five things that allow me to concentrate on creative activity are: 1. time to myself 2. freedom from guilt 3. space or place to do my own work 4. emotional support 5. love.

Those who create obstacles to my having these are: 1. myself 2. Barbara 3. Douglas 4. Ryan. Naturally, I give myself the least amount of time and all the rest of them—I jump at their slightest need.

My unrestrained creativity would cause the greatest danger to . . . me! I would die of guilt. Guilt over not attending everyone else's needs. And fear. Fear at the being overwhelmed by the sheer presence of my feelings.

Assignment: Write a scene in which all your creative "allowances" have been taken away. What do you do with yourself?

Example: I am locked in a small dark room with no windows, no light, no yard, no trees. It has no space where I can spread out, no place—for my books, my PC, for my music. The music would bounce against the walls with horrid reverberation.

I'm alone in this bleak place. No one is here to love me or support my efforts. I don't mean financially, but with words, a touch, a hug, a smile. I can't make it. I can't create. I am in a vacuum. My brain is shredded. Without light, love, space, I am totally void.

Assignment: Write a scene in which you confront the greatest obstacle to your creativity. Are you torn with guilt or filled

with anticipation? What are your feelings and the consequences of your actions?

Example: The lack of space is the greatest obstacle to my
creativity. But what kind of space? Is it space/time from the
people I feel obligated to or space to move around in? Is it
human or physical? It's both!

I need airy, sunlit space. This is freedom! A sunlit space
with love and support. I could draw, write, and speak with
these tools! But the fucking asshole has taken these tools
from me! She has cramped my creativity. This is my worst
nightmare, and I have manifested it.

I might as well cover everything I see in black, drape a shroud
over my PC, draw a curtain across the bookshelves. Anything I
desire, she has stripped me of. Creation—fuck, no way! My
thoughts are of death, walking skeletons. Not even white ones,
but ugly black skeletons with skin fragments left on the bones.

Maybe death is creation. Maybe we should all . . . NO! I
can't feel this way. I desire peace, tranquility, soft music,
vibrant colors, billowing curtains. Lift the fog. Be dead, but
come back as I create you. My love, my support. Because I am
the creator of you, my love.

Review: How did these prospects affect you? Which was
harder—anticipating the confrontations necessary to getting
what you need to nourish your creativity or facing the room of
your own with the empty canvas or blank ream of writing
paper? Write about these apprehensions.

Imagination Is the Healing Tool

HEALING—AND ART—occurs when we transform a fixed
image into a dynamic image, into a literally or energetically moving

picture. We then recognize how we have been the lead character in our own production as well as the lighting director, casting director, location scout, and set designer. We see that we have always been the one who edited the script and the photography and froze those frames in which our wounds occurred. We fixed the trauma, disappointment, or grief in our subconscious minds and in our bodies. And it is we who have the power to release it all.

In our writing, we recast the drama, relocate the film, rearrange the set, and rewrite as much of the script as we need. Of course we can't change history, but we can change our perspective toward it and therefore its power over us.

Introspection, the very point of *Writing As a Healing Art,* nourishes self-awareness while expression gives shape and voice to our revelations. Look at the role one student, a former actress, in fact, realized she had created for herself:

> I am not as tired as I pretend to be. I realize that I use the tremendous amount of work I do as a shield against pleasure and intimacy. I also use it to protect myself from other people's anger—after all, how in the world can you be angry at someone who works so damned hard and who is so damned tired?
>
> I thought I was looking for a caretaker. Now, as I write, I realize that's not true anymore. I don't believe I could allow someone to take care of me. After all, I'm eminently able to take care of myself—and others as well.
>
> I've made a Russian opera of my life. A role played in the Grand Opera style—overblown, overdramatized, and a lousy act at that, because I've used the role badly. It seems the only thing I'm tired of is pretending.

The more we write, the more attuned we become to all sensation. Our insights become more immediate, our perceptions more pointed, and our expressions more direct. When we consciously allow the mind to speak through the body, we gain diagnostic power. We begin to acknowledge our intuition as sensory intelligence.

The Mouth Speaks, the Writing Hand Hears

You inform yourself by hearing what you tell others.

—ALINA PANTERA, teacher

WHAT WE GIVE out is what we want most, and when it is advice or help, it's usually that which we ourselves need. Not only do we write the story we live, we also selectively hear it. *Writing As a Healing Art* dissolves that selectivity. By connecting us directly to the subconscious, it allows us to hear our "true" voice.

Mind and Mouth

Assignment: Like the mind-mouth exercise you did in chapter 6, write a word-for-word account of another unpleasant encounter (or part of a conversation) that pushed your buttons. Again, first record only the words that were spoken. Then, recount the conversation, including the voice that was speaking in your mind and/or the one you imagine was speaking in the other person's mind.

Example:
HIM: Hi. It's me, Dave.
ME: Hey, can you hold on? I'm on the other line.
HIM: Well, I just wanted to know if you got my message the other night.
ME: Yeah, I got it, but not until the next day.
HIM: Well, you *could* have called me back.

Me: What, to tell you I wasn't in and not to come over? It was *already* the next day when I picked up the message.

Him: Well, you could have *at least* called back.

Me: I'm sorry. And I'm on the other line. I'll have to talk to you later.

Now, don't hold back. Let the chatterbox in your head squawk—and record every word you both were thinking. Exaggerate freely.

Him: Hi. It's me. Dave. (You lousy bitch. I haven't heard from you all week. What the hell kind of friend do you call yourself!)

Me: Hey, can you hold on? I'm on the other line.

Him: Well, I just wanted to know if you got my message the other night. (How dare you ignore me when I call and offer to come over. I extend myself and this is all the appreciation I get?)

Me: Yeah, I got it. But not until the next day. (Jesus Christ, this was five days ago. What the hell is this *really* all about? I don't have time for this bullshit.)

Him: Well, you *could* have called me back (you treacherous, no-good excuse for a friend).

Me: What, to tell you I wasn't in and not to come over? It was *already* the next day when I picked up the message (for Christ's sake!).

Him: Well, you could have *at least* called back. (I'll make you sorry for ignoring me, you bastard. I'll make you sorry. I'll show you for the useless traitor you are.)

Me: I'm sorry. (No I'm not. Who am I kidding? This guy is nothing more than a self-absorbed, selfish little shit. Doesn't he have an elderly parent to take care of or a kid to raise or a charity to support. Get a life, schmuck! And stop annoying me with your narcissistic pettiness! Whatever . . . I don't want to waste another second of my time or energy on this bullshit.) And I'm on the other line. I'll have to talk to you later (but not for a bloody long time, if ever, asshole!).

Review: How did the tone of your oral and mental voices compare? How long after the encounter did the voice in your head continue the conversation? How long after *writing out* the second version did the voice in your head continue? Was writing it out effective at shutting it up?

Example: The mental voice was sure a lot more honest. But the actual voice was to the point. I was proud of myself for that. The tone of my oral voice was much more diplomatic. Cheery, patient, even-tempered. The mental voices were both biting, nasty, sparring, swords drawn.

The oral conversation kept playing in my head for hours! It really pushed my buttons. I wanted to throttle him, the twit! I was even getting riled about it days later. But once I sat down and did the exercise, I felt like I'd finished a fencing match. Touché! And walked off the mat. I also felt much more prepared to let the imaginary voice out—fuck the diplomat and welcome the dragon slayer! Fuck Dave, too.

Review: Was it easier or harder than you expected to remember the words you used and heard? Which was easier—writing what you said or what you heard?

Assignment: Write out your confrontation scene from above as if the other person were huge and you were small. Then reverse the scale, and make yourself enormous and your confronter small.

Review: How did the change in scale affect your feelings about yourself and about the other person? Write about "When I feel big." Write about "When I feel small."

Assignment: Write out the same scene, this time describing yourself in full, glowing panoramic color and the confronter in two-dimensional black and white. Then again reverse the devices, notice the effects, and write about them.

———————

Once you hear your true stories—the ones *behind* your words as well as *in* the words—your communications gain power. You will be better able to say what you really mean because you are better able to distinguish between the stories in your head and the events in your present. Sometimes they are congruent. Often they have nothing to do with one another.

We serve others as well as ourselves when we learn to distinguish the mouth from the mind. We gain a greater ability to *not get enrolled* in others' stories. We understand whose story we are fostering—theirs or our own. Our writing teaches us to be more sympathetic to and less identified with others' confusion or suffering. We learn to reflect rather than to perpetuate.

A more accurate means of evaluating someone's condition or intent is to examine their affect and aura and to listen to their timbre and tone. In other words, what are their body and energy telling you?

The Body Speaks, the Writing Hand Hears

Original thought is the product not of the brain, but of the full self.

—ROBERT GRUDIN, *The Grace of Great Things*

THE MORE YOU write, the more acute your awareness grows to bodily changes or sensations that occur from "touching" on certain subjects. The more you allow these feelings to expand into full pictures, complete with sound, touch, taste, smell, and sight, the more freely your creativity flows. When you let the images lead you back to where and when you first experienced them, your writing experience becomes, as one student described, "like Howard Carter's first glimpse into King Tut's tomb must have been. After digging around for years, you discover a real opening. At first your eyes can focus only on one small spot in the darkness. Then as you become accustomed to the light, your vision expands. Whole rooms reveal themselves in amazing clarity."

Years after his surgery for a brain tumor, one student wrote about the anger his "bruised brain" expressed:

They drilled a hole through my brain, and my brain was bruised. Now a part of my stomach fills the little hole in my brain, to hold the rest of it in place. HA! Mother was always afraid I would turn out to be just like Daddy—another bruised brain. Another tormented soul. Institutionalized for 36 years. Will that happen to me? Is that what happens to all bruised brains? They get locked away with Mother's signature on the consent papers.

My fear returned big time when I spoke to Mother on the phone, describing my present life. She lamented not sharing the holidays with me, and I said, "You can come to here, to me." I heard her brain thinking out loud. She was impressed with the invitation.

The next morning I awoke in a panic. She could come and lock me away. After the family conference, of course. The whole family will convene and lock me away. Don't they understand? The bruise is healed.

For years, during times of crisis, I used to experience a terrible, heavy constriction not exactly in, but on, my chest. In my imagination, a frozen garden claw, the kind used to pull weeds out of the ground, was penetrating my breastplate and pounding on my heart like a fist. I referred to the feeling as "the icy claw." During one particular crisis, I called a hypnotherapist friend for help. He reminded me that the power of the icy claw came not from the circumstances involved in my crisis but instead from my own imagination. "But what about this fist on my chest!" I cried, insulted by his lack of sympathy. "Laura, there *is* no fist on your chest," he reminded me. "Melt the image."

Once I got over my indignation (after all, I'd called *him* so *he* could take the icy claw away), I got to work on my own revision. Once I was no longer fixated on the icy claw, I was able to focus on the elements of my crisis . . . and regain the power to deal with it.

Recovery from trauma is accelerated by the victim's ability to recount the events and thereby release their emotional hold on the physical body. This was dramatized in my class when one of my students, who had been held up at gunpoint during a weekly Quaker meeting, found herself too emotionally paralyzed by fright to even describe the event to her husband or discuss it with the victims. To help her provide a starting point, I asked her first to focus specifically on the gun and then to write about the taste and the smell of her fear. Here are some of the writings she produced:

The Big Gun

This gun really had my attention. It was suddenly there with some guy attached to the back end of it. The wood was beautiful and there was a lot of it. It was the brightest thing in the room. It was a honey chestnut/cherry burl lacquered shiny smooth piece of wood. Its function was not immediately apparent, nor the man behind. The wood was pretty. But it was a gun, and it had a barrel that extended only a short distance past the wood. A nice finish job. The hole was big. The wood was big, and it could put a very big hole in me and splatter my guts or heart or lungs or whatever organs it hit against the far wall or all over Eric who would also get a big hole in him. Stop camera, stop action. Bad direction. This is not allowed to happen and doesn't have to. Just everybody stay relaxed. Mellow, very mellow. Guns aren't mellow. That gun was heavy and orange and had a big hole for a big bullet and could make a very loud sound and scare us to death so that we would throw up and die.

The Taste of Fear

Fear tastes like metal. Like metal melting up from beneath my tongue sliding up and over my gums and teeth and fillings where it recognizes itself and jumps up and down shouting METAL! I've found you! Metal! Metal! Metal! The taste of fear slips between my lips and drools down my chin. I spit. Ptooey. The taste of fear is deep and wide and splits my trust like firewood, dried and stacked and protected and now CRACK! Split and splintered and ready for the fire. The taste of fear is the salt I imagine on Mary's leg as I hold on for dear life—or death—or what is to be. . . . I want to lick her leg. I want to taste the salt. I want her to be alive. I want to know that I am alive.

The Smell of Fear

The smell of fear is empty, slow, and vacant. There is no smell because this isn't real enough to have a smell. No molecules are moving around on no breeze between no entities that don't connect. This man has no smell. He is, however, human. He is afraid, nervous. Dangerously nervous. We have stunned him as he has us. And we cannot connect. Not right away. Therefore, no smell. Just a hologram until my eyes make their way through to something, but still no smell. We are all like deer in the headlights in the winter. No smell. Time too thick for such a delicate interaction, for such a current. Slow current taking the messages back and forth and around. Barely functioning. Hard to communicate. What does he want? What is he trying to do. He's fumbling at this and it's making him nervous, and so, becoming more real, more frightening, more frightened. Finger twitching or jiggling the trigger. Big gun. No smell. No powder or sulphur or sweat or cologne or filth. Nothing. The rug smelled like Jane's dog. Now I remember what the fear of that moment smelled like. Mildew and dog and feet.

Sensations of Fear

Assignment: You are having an anxiety attack or trauma. Write about where in your body the anxiety or fear attacks you. Make your description big, blatant, aggressive.

Example: It's hard to breathe and I'm slightly nauseous. My stomach is as hard as a rock. My shoulders feel like they're nailed to my chest, and my arms feel like dying butterflies nailed to the nail that nails my chest. I sense that moving my arms and legs will liberate me—but my chest is rigid as the trunk of a tree, and I know liberation won't come from anywhere except the chest. My chest is a tree, and I'm chained to it. Me, the lumberjack who can't even bring myself down to the ground.

Assignment: Describe the taste, smell, and color of your fear. Describe the color of fear you have perceived in others when in states of crisis.

Start anywhere in writing about trauma. Even if it is writing about how your hand is shaking so hard you don't believe you can even write. Write about the shaking. You can use any sensation or point of view as a means of entering a recollection and reclaiming your power over it.

Your Point of View Determines Your Power

> The realization that viewpoint plays a central role in
> how we experience events underlies much of mod-
> ern thought. It accounts in part for the multiple sur-
> faces in Picasso's Cubism, the multiple narrators in
> Faulkner's novels, and the Lorentz transformations in
> Einstein's special theory of relativity.
>
> —RICHARD SCHWARTZ, PH.D., *Cold War Reference Guide*

YOUR STORIES' POWER to run your life diminishes as you gain recognition of your authorship. The more you explore your stories from different points of view, the more detached you grow from your own fixed points of view and the more power you gain.

Here is an example written by a student, an actor whose father had never, in the student's entire acting career, come to watch him perform. Every time the student walked on stage, he habitually imagined his father sitting in the audience . . . scrutinizing him. Writing the scene out from the point of view of his father's mind and eyes released him from his emotional and creative captivity:

I knew he couldn't do this. Look at that, the boy's not nearly as good as the rest of the cast. He keeps missing his cues and miss-ing his marks. Good God, he must be so embarrassed—I'm embarrassed for him. That's why I never wanted to come. It's embarrassing for me! I'm ashamed this kid is my own.

My son, up there, making a fool of himself. Looking inept, inept and unkempt. Why the hell can't he ever look right—get a haircut, wear pants that fit. Wear clothes that don't look like they came from the Salvation Army. Why can't he ever look PRESENTABLE! Respectable. And now that he's gained so much weight—he says it's for this role. Whoever heard of such nonsense!

Deliberately gaining weight for a stage part. Doesn't he know how hard it is to get rid of? Look what I had to do to knock off ten pounds. Cutting out the booze was the toughest part. Damn, I could use a drink right now. Love to leap out of this seat and go toss one back. Make a few phone calls. Set up a golf date.

That whole trip to Scotland—five days of golf—and it rains. The whole time. Gotta work out my schedule so I can get over there again soon. Maybe after the merger. Gotta call Frank. Go over the numbers one more time. Before I leave for the coast. I hope Stephanie remembered to make reservations at Pantino's. What act is this? I've got to try to reach Andrew before he leaves the country. Isn't this performance thing over yet!

Putting Out

Assignment: Write a response to the question "What do I have to put out to get what I want?"

Example: What do I have to put out to get what I want? Put out or put down? I used to think I had to be a charity case to get what I wanted. To be on the Neediest Cases Christmas List. Then, who could deny me? Pitiful, but oh-so-deserving me.

It used to be good grades. Where did that get me? Nowhere. Not once in my entire career has anyone ever asked for my school or college transcripts. Of course Mother taught me it was a happy face. Put on a happy face, don't wear your heart on your sleeve. Recently I got impetigo on my face from working in the garden. It looked angry and red, like the unrelenting acne of my adolescence. The acre whose scars are still evident on my "ruined" brow. I wrote *acre* when I meant to write *acne,* but yeah, it feels like an acre. My acre of land, acre of hope, acre of dreams. They lie in art, my dreams do. Where all transformation lies. Aha! That's what I have to put out to get what I want. My art.

Not my cunt or my wallet or my sympathy or all my resources and all my energy. I don't have to exhaust myself to get what I want. What I have to put out is what I want most. I want peace of mind and luxuriance in expression. The luxuriance of creation. The luxuriance of being fully in my body.

If I don't want to put out, I don't have to. I don't have to. I don't. I don't. I won't be punished if I don't put out. But maybe I will be if I do. Will I be punished for putting out or for not putting out enough? Do I have to be punished or published? Or are they they same?

Another student wrote it this way:

Example: Put out? Well, I *do* put out . . . and why buy the milk if the cow is free? Or whatever that saying is. It's just that I *like* putting out. Not putting out would be playing a silly, childish mind game. But I'm not actually putting out. I'm taking in— ahhhh, great smile across my face as I envelop all men—take them in to my warm and welcoming arms, rest their heads against my bosom, swallow them whole within my moist darkness. Put out? No. What do I have to *take in* to get what I want?

Flexibility in point of view increases your ability to expand your options. You recognize more entrances, exits, and opportunities than any fixed perspective allows. Observing from numerous points of view makes you more energetically available to unexpected twists and turns in your writing and to change and healing in your life.

Recognizing Your Stories Through Metaphor

> Some of the best inventions of humanity are models
> of the body and brain. For me, the book is metaphor-
> ically bodylike—the spine, the symmetry, the cover,
> the contents. Because of that, the book has an
> attractive potential for subverting the usual and
> artificial division between the mind and the body,
> which I believe are one.
>
> —RICHARD TUTTLE, artist

JUST AS FREUD liberated the content of dreams from the realm of the subconscious, the writing technique taught in this book works with metaphor to reflect hidden thoughts and bring them to your awareness. Recognition of metaphors and their meanings enables you to see the outer world more clearly as a mirror of your inner world, and any part of your life as a microcosm of your whole life.

Power mediates between our internal and external worlds, and as it does so, it communicates in a language of myth and symbol. Through such visionary work as this writing process, dreams and myths grow more meaningful. A dream, as Joseph Campbell defined it, is "a personal experience of that deep dark ground that is the support of our conscious lives." Myths are society's dreams. Archetypal dreams are personal dreams of mythic dimension— dreams that come directly to the conscious mind from the soul.

As your ability to interpret develops, you will find yourself better able to head the messages your body and your subconscious are continually sending. "Healing from any illness is facilitated by identifying your symbols," explains Caroline Myss, noted diagnostic intuitive. Similarly, you will more readily recognize your personal metaphors and their measure of power.

When one of my students, the owner of a small business, expressed his discomfort over his preoccupation with the stock market, I asked him to enlarge his concern into an obsession and become completely consumed, in his writing, with his investments. He wrote:

I Am the Bull Market

So identified am I with this aged and moribund bull market that *I have become the bull.* The volatile life force of collective commerce is my Taurian prana. I am plugged in for the duration as if on some tenuous life support. Financial hucksters and economic pundits are my physicians and diagnosticians. Market statistics track my vital signs. The opening and closing bells are my systolic and diastolic rhythms as upticks and downticks mark the skittish arhythmias of my cloven syncopation. Fear and greed roil my gut while horns of dilemmas etch an ever inconclusive EEG.

I then asked the student to completely reverse the identification. He wrote:

I Am Not My Money

Horrified, I awake one morning to find that I am not my money. I do not unfurl like a wad of tightly rolled banknotes as I rise from the blankets. Ominously, the radio alarm is blaring the Desiderata instead of stock quotes.

I climb into trousers and reach for the comfort of the change on the dresser. I am aghast as my pockets zip shut like sutured lacerations and coins roll to the floor and out the door in unseemly agitation. My beloved wallet has metamorphosed into a doe-eyed gerbil that regards me placidly as it nests in a confetti of shredded ATM slips. Meanwhile, my long-suffering checkbook has bounced out the window, finally committing suicide.

In a crisis of identity, I call for help whereupon I am dismissed as an imposter by my financial adviser. "You, sir, are not your money," he avers. "What am I then?" I plead. "A child of the universe, nothing more, nothing less," he assures me as he blithely expropriates my managed assets.

Everything Is a Metaphor

The following eight exercises are intended to make you more mindful of how you express your feelings about your life in seemingly mundane contexts. Each subject is, in its own way, a self-portrait. It is important that you write out every one of these examples, although not necessarily all at once. With each exercise the extent of your self-projection—and its power—will be made clearer.

Assignment: Describe the contents and condition of your refrigerator, beginning with its character. Is it a virtual medicine chest of supplements and remedies, a cornucopia of the earth's harvest, an adolescent's junk-food heaven, or a fast-food pit stop? As you write, be mindful of what feelings the thought of your refrigerator prompts—apprehension, delight, addictive anticipation, resignation, numbness? Where do these feelings occur—in your throat, stomach, teeth, heart?

Review:

- How much of the contents are for the purpose of comforting you or offering compensation for unhappy feelings?

- How much is there strictly for the purpose of nutrition?

- How much represents your willingness to nurture yourself?

Assignment: Describe the contents of your bedroom closet beginning with the feelings you have as you approach it. Are you apprehensive over encountering the chaos within or excited over reviewing your fabulous wardrobe? Is it stuffed or spare, organized or messy? How often do you reorganize it, and add or remove things from it? How would your mother describe it?

Review:

- How much of the contents reflects the past?

- How much reflects an anticipated life?

- What percentage of your time do you give to acquiring and maintaining it?

- Are you hard or gentle on your clothes?

- What are your favorite pieces of clothing? Do you wear them often or rarely?

- How much color does your closet contain?

- How do you *feel* in your "work" clothes, and how much time do you spend in them?

- What else do you "keep in the closet"?

- What do you most want to bring out of the closet?

Assignment: Describe your car: Did you choose it for comfort, economy, practicality, speed, safety, or fun, or did you select it for pure style? How do you feel about yourself when you're driving it? Do you attend faithfully to its maintenance? Is it scrupulously clean inside, relatively cluttered, or does it smell like a wet dog?

Review:

• What do you think someone observing you in your car thinks of you? In other words, as a portrait of you, what picture does your car paint?

• How often do others ride in it with you? Who are your favorite passengers? How often are they with you?

• Do you like being in your car? What is your ideal car? If you don't own it now, do you anticipate owning it ever? When?

Assignment: Is your furniture basically an anonymous part of the scenery, or do you give it great attention? Describe its style, condition, color, and arrangement. Where did you acquire it, and how long did it take? What's the greatest amount of money you've ever spent on a piece of furniture or art? Are there pieces you'd like to get rid of? If so, how long have you been thinking about doing this? Are there pieces you'd like to acquire? If so, do you know exactly what they are and where you'll get them, or is your notion still unformed? What is your favorite place to shop for furniture, and why? How often do you rearrange your furniture or reupholster it? Do you look at books and magazines or to professionals for ideas and advice?

Review:

• How closely does your taste in furniture resemble that which you grew up with?

- What does your mother think of your taste? How does that make you feel?

- What picture does your furniture paint about you—that you live like a graduate student whose mature life lies in the future, a suburban bourgeois, a bohemian with little concern for the material, a highly invested sophisticate, or someone who cares a lot but doesn't know how to put it together?

- How does this picture compare with the one you have of yourself? Of the picture you wish to project?

Assignment: Apply the same approach as above to writing about your yard, garden, or indoor plants.

Review:

- What does this say about your interest in interacting with nature? In cultivation? In controlling nature or encouraging wildness?

- Is your garden functional, ornamental, or just there?

- How much does it resemble what it was when you moved in?

- Do you like being in it, or do you essentially ignore it?

- What picture does it paint about you? How closely does that picture resemble who you are or how you wish to be perceived.

Assignment: Apply the same approach as above to writing about your work environment. What is its quality of comfort, visual appeal, practicality? What would you change about it?

Review: How much control do you have over putting those changes into effect? How many people share your work space? What percentage of your time do you spend in this environment?

Assignment: Write about your hands: Are they bony, shapely, blunt, strong, delicate, flaccid, deft, expressive, big? What is the condition of your nails? How much attention and money do you spend on them? What are the most memorable hands you remember? Describe the hands of your parents, siblings, lover, spouse, children, closest friends.

Assignment: Write about the part of your body you dislike most. When did you first feel this way about this part of your body? How important is it to you to change it? Are you willing or not to spend the time, energy, and money? What would change most in your life with this improvement? Who would be most pleased and displeased by this change? How many people do you know who feel similarly about their own bodies? How many times a day do you look in the mirror?

———————

These exercises are great training for detective work. As you see what they reflect about your own inner life, you will recognize the wealth of information they offer you about others. Use them—without judgment—to fill out profiles of those around you, to gain understanding of people with whom you interact. Every aspect of people's possessions and homes tells a whole story.

CHAPTER ELEVEN

Re-creating Your Stories Through Art

I start out slowly, choppy, timidly . . . recording facts

and data. Then the flow of sentences carries me away

from myself, down the stream and around the bend to

a new reality. Here come the verbs and nouns, the

consequence. Reaction, retreat, reflection. This is a

song—my story—and with its singing I am changed.

—GERRY GRANT, writing student

ALL ART DRAWS upon a variety of devices to impart feeling and create focus. Among these devices are scale, texture, proportion, materials, color, cadence, point of view, and vocabulary (verbal and visual). Modification of any one, to any degree, creates shifts in depth and in meaning.

Consider, for example, the type of film chosen for a movie. Black-and-white film immediately conveys the fact-oriented sense of a documentary or the suspenseful ambience of film noir. Technicolor, on the other hand, creates a lushly romantic sensibility. *The Wizard of Oz* is a perfect example of how the contrast between black and white and Technicolor enhanced the story. Think how the contrast between the grimness of Kansas and the magic of Oz are emphasized by the use of the two different film types.

In sculpture, the size of the object and the choice of materials determine much about the object's impact. Consider the difference in effect between a monument carved in stone and a miniature blown in glass.

The following exercises demonstrate how meaning can be affected by any device in any medium. I advise you to first read the instructions and then allow yourself time to totally indulge your imagination. This part of the exercise is strictly mental—no writing, no notes.

In the second part of the exercise, after you have developed as much imaginary material as you wish, begin writing—descriptions, impressions, physical reactions, emotional feelings, questions, and revelations.

Film

WHILE ALL ART, by nature, can be powerfully cathartic, film is the form in which expression of emotions and release of tension are most often experienced today. By watching the struggles of characters on screen, we relive and relieve our own issues and conflicts. We can regard their choices, observe their actions and reactions, project our own longings, and weep or triumph with them. In fact, one great measure of a film's success is its cathartic ability. When we come out of the theater or away from a video feeling in some way changed or seeing our lives or others' differently, we have more than simply viewed a movie. We have experienced the power of art.

Your Life Is a Disaster Film

Assignment: Describe an issue, question, problem, or fear from your own life as if it were a disaster film. Where does the action begin—with a tight, but telling, shot of a meaningful detail or a wide expanse of horizon? Is there a sound track? Choose actors for your story as if you were actually casting the film. Who plays you, your mother, your father, your boss, your lover? Who in the story gets saved and who perishes?

Assignment: Reverse the plot and kill off those who lived and save the others.

Review: How did it feel to imagine your life on the big screen being viewed by millions? Did you find yourself holding your breath at any particular parts? How did the two different endings make you feel, and where in your body did you feel it?

Assignment: Use the story of your first sexual experience again. First describe it as if it were a photo album you were paging through. What is the character and quality of this album and of the pictures themselves? What is the signature image of the collection, the one you would chose for the cover?

Example: It's an old album, like something from the forties or fifties. The photos are black and white and have those squiggly edges. They're affixed with the triangular corners that come off in the old family photo albums when the paste wears out.

The first photo (which is also the cover photo on the album) is a close-up of my face. I look scared. The second is of the girl, shot from the waist up. Her top is off, and she's looking hard and ready and somewhat bored. The third photo shows me on top of her. The heads you see are the back of mine, the front of hers looking up at the ceiling, still bored.

The fourth picture is very blurred—it shows my buttocks humping. Her legs are splayed unattractively.

In the fifth photo, you see me sitting at the edge of the bed with my head in my hands and her standing over me, looking down and somewhat irritated. The sixth photo is of the empty dorm room—the door closed. This picture is torn, ripped apart. Only fragments of it remain in the album.

Assignment: Visualize these images in motion, on a movie screen. What is the title of this film, who do you see as its director, and what actor is playing your role? Set the movie in a different location and add a sound track. Increase the volume until you drown out the dialogue. Replay the scene without music and with only dialogue. Turn the film into a fantasy, changing your partner into a totally different person, and completely transform the ending.

Dance and Music

DANCERS WORK TO develop balance, physical strength, flexibility, and responsiveness to rhythm. They need command of both bodily and facial gesture. Yet choreography comes most alive when a dancer, having absorbed all these but concentrating on none, relies on muscle memory, musicality, and pure rhythmic response. The same occurs in writing after we absorb the patterns, rhythms, and images of our thoughts. When they dance from the subconscious to the page via our hands, they perform with a power that exalts far beyond any disciplined recitation of facts.

Pas de Deux . . . or Trois . . . or . . .

Assignment: You are about to stage your first-sex story as a dance or music performance. What music will it be danced to—blues, jazz, a rhapsody, a dirge or Beethoven's *Fifth*? Who will fill out the chorus? Is the *pas de deux* (or ménage à trois or whatever) slow and elegiac, an orgy of acid rock, a melodramatic Barbra Streisand torch song, or a production out of a Hollywood extravaganza? Who will you cast as your dance partner? Who will you have dance your role?

Example: I would cast this failed *pas de deux* with a *film noir* siren like Gene Tierney as the female role and a nerdy guy like Leslie Howard . . . no, Tom Ewell in *Seven Year Itch* would play me. The music is dissonant, something like a Charles Ives symphony with forceful Sousa-like beginnings, but later, atonal and confused. There would be alternations of strong horns, followed by a dirge-like low droning. Or maybe it would be Stockhausen, who is even more dissonant and random. Anyway, the music has no structure, just sequential noise.

The coda would be the more depressing repetitive pieces by Philip Glass minus the interesting cumulative drama his music can sometimes evoke: low three-note phrases, with little variation, fading out into flaccid oblivion.

As a matter of fact, for years after, I had massive flaccid oblivion nightmares. It's a good thing I became gay.

Literature, Drama, and Poetry

The cadence of language is inseparable from the
words. Words can lie, but their music betrays the
soul. The truth is in the hearing.

—GERRY GRANT, writing student

MYTHS AND FAIRY tales appeal directly to the right brain—the creative, intuitive, nonlogical, nonanalytical side of the brain. This is why children respond to them so readily: A child's neurological system is still closely resonant with the ethereal.

Likewise, poetry draws its visual and emotive power from the right brain, which is expressed through cadence and sometimes rhyme to the left brain. Fiction is born of the right brain, nonfiction derives from the left. This is why undirected, right-brain writing has such power. It puts you in touch with experience. It transports you.

Through dialect and cadence, both drama and literature appeal to the right brain and draw us into the world of the imagination. One student wrote about her difficulty in understanding a book of short stories. Only when she allowed herself to "hear" them did they come alive—and become deeply meaningful. She wrote:

My sister gave me a book of Grace Paley stories. I had never read this writer before nor heard her speak, and I was having the greatest trouble making sense at all of what I was reading. I couldn't understand what my problem was.

After all, I enjoy short stories, and if my sister had recommended this writer, then she must be skilled.

I had to reread whole pages, looking back to figure out references to pronouns and even verbs. It was frustrating, and I was about to give up when the description of neighborhood (or was it a character?) gave me a clue.

The book was set in New York, in a Jewish immigrant ghetto. Aha! I began reading with a Jewish accent and inflection. Magic! I started the book over from the beginning . . . and couldn't put it down. I was captured—laughing and hollering, wondering and complaining, realizing the world right along with the characters.

I could hear the noises of the city and the cooking smells that wafted from open windows. I could feel the sweat in the sticky summer heat. What fun! The inflection, the cadence, the rhythm had opened the door to the writing.

Years later I heard Grace Paley speak at a peace demonstration. She is a dedicated activist, like I am. Remembering the difficulty I had had when I didn't recognize her music, I bent over laughing.

Indeed, cadence can be thought of as the music of words. While vocabulary intimates or delineates a thought, cadence amplifies or contradicts it through rhythmic force. A student's repetition of a simple phrase dramatically contrasts with complex horror in this scene:

Damn you. I held his hand, forcing it away from my face. Damn you, I thought through clenched teeth.

My back tightens, straightens, strengthens. His leg forces me back. I twist. My hands grab at his, my teeth bite at any flesh they touch. I kick.

Damn you. Down to the ground. Leaves, falling leaves, beautiful colors, dark and dirty from the rain. My face pushed into the dirt.

Damn you. I turn, twist. Face to face. He needs his hands to pull off my clothes. I use my hands to shove back his head. I use my back and arm like an Egyptian lever. We strain at each other. I want up. He wants down.

He slips on the wet leaves. God and nature gave me the edge. We fall to the ground. His legs still around mine, but now our bodies are side to side. And I have a hand free.

Damn you. The rock is heavy. It crushes his skull. Damn you. I heave the rock again. Damn you. I get up. Grab my bike and ride away. Damn you. Dead you.

The cadence of writing responds to its subject and mood. One student discovered how her writing "takes on a certain rhythm or style according to what I felt at the time of the event I'm describing. For example, when I write about my childhood, the writing simplifies. I find myself using words a child could understand. When I'm trying to figure out a problem or feeling, the vocabulary and sentence structure begin to sound like a mystery novel. And if I'm trying to get a point across to someone else (which usually means I'm trying to convince myself), the style becomes evangelistic, commanding, emotional, and assured."

Consider the power of the cadence in the writing of a student whom I asked to describe a scene of total incapacity:

> I lie here. I feel it coming. Warm, full, a trickle, a movement, a flow, from my back, from my rear, out, escaping between my legs, beneath my rear, under my back, puddling. Warm, cool, cold wetness. Cold, sticky, stinging.
>
>   She comes. Rolls me left. Takes the sheet. Rolls me right. Rolls me left. Puts down the sheet. Rolls me right. She leaves. She returns. Rolls me left. Cocks my leg. Wipes. Cold, clean wipes. Metal clicks, pushes, spreads. Plastic tubes push, punch, push. Metal clicks. Wipes. Cold, clean wipes. Rolls me right.

When we are conscious of the scale, texture, color, cadence, and visual vocabulary in our writing, we can reduce or enlarge, fortify or deplete the power of any image or situation.

The same student who wrote the piece above evoked the bitterness that edged her family's Christmas celebrations by using accounts of food and the "taste of words."

Sweet Hostilities

Christmas at Lois's. Goodies all over. Angel candy, chocolate chip cookies, for dinner ravioli with butter sauce, wine, and raspberry slushes, all swimming inside of me. It's Christmas. I must be nice. Lois commands, "Dear, try the Angel candy. Giovanni's don't carry it no more. I had to make it myself. Do you realize how hard it is to make? Beating the egg whites. My poor hands. I'm getting old. I won't be here much longer. The arthritis is so painful. You must try the Angel candy."

Lois, 72, going on 102, and more durable than ever. She'll outlive me. She outlived Everis. She killed him with her food. Maybe she's trying to kill me. Be nice. It's Christmas.

Kate wants to bake cookies with Grandma. Chocolate chip. Ginger snaps. Sugar cookies—covered with sugar, made with sugar, red and green sugar dripping through my veins, making my head throb. I hate cookies. Sure Sweetie, Mommie will try another cookie. A Christmas tree cookie with red candy balls on each branch. Oh, how wonderful.

Motivation and action also can be effectively conveyed through dialogue. In the following two writing examples that use primarily dialogue, one student expresses the unrelenting demands of motherhood and matrimony while another humorously communicates his philosophy of temptation.

On April 7, 1988, Beth Gave Birth to Me

Mommie! Mommie, there's swimming today. Where's my swimsuit? Where's the Mickey and Goofy towel? Where's my pink top and skirt?

Mommie! Get up. Wake up. I'm hungry. Can I watch TV? Can I let the puppy in? Mommie, Bibi's chasing the rabbit.

Mommie, you need to call Mrs. Pappas. Kiki and I want a play date tomorrow. You have to sign this. Miss Brewster says this is due today. Where are my shoes? Did you call for an appointment? My bangs are too long. Can you curl my hair now? The puppy is throwing up on the rug.

I need a can to bring to Girl Scouts. Can I get a costume like Kiki's for Halloween? I told Miss Brewster you'd bake cookies for Halloween. Miss Frances wants you to program the Accelerated Reader list for us.

Can I get some money out of your purse? I want to buy a Yikes pencil. Kiki has folders with animals on them. Can we go to Kmart after school? Mommie, where are my socks?

"Dear, don't forget to tell Charles Schwab to go ahead with the purchase of the Disney stocks for Beth's account. Oh, by the way, buy some Mattel while you're at it."

The Devil Made Me Do It

Connie just laughed when I told her that the Devil made me do it.

No shit. He was sitting right there, where you are, when I got up for work, I told her. I was trying to sleep, but the damned dog next door kept barking, and I finally gave up.

Scared the shit out of me at first.

I mean, I walked out into the living room, and there was this naked red guy sitting at the table, stirring a cup of coffee with his finger and barking just like the damned dog.

Then I recognized him.

"Oh, it's you," I said. "Didn't you ever hear of knocking?"

"You mean like, I stand at the door and knock? Or do you mean like, 'Knock, knock. Who's there?'"

"And you're using my favorite cup!"

"Relax, pour one for yourself," he said.

"Thanks I need it. Now that you're here, would you like something to eat. I've been doing pancakes lately."

"Pancakes? Uh, no thanks. I had a county commissioner, a

CPA, and two lawyers on the way over."

I was getting worried again. This guy doesn't show up just to be sociable. Did I welch on some deal or commit some major Sin of Omission (my favorite kind)? Anyway, I decided to play it cool.

"CPA? You're doing accountants lately? You must be getting hard up."

"Not at all. This guy worked for a commissioner."

"Oh."

"It was really a nice piece of work. I found them together in a crack house downtown. One gulp. No prob. I gave them heart attacks, but made it look like foul play, just for the fun of it."

"Did anyone ever tell you you're a really twisted individual?"

"Yeah, I hear that all the time. I'm used to it."

He stirred his coffee again, and it steamed as if the stirring made it better. He looked up at me and grinned.

"Okay, Okay, I'll bite. WHAT BRINGS YOU HERE?"

"Thought you'd never ask. Guess!"

"Aw shit, man. We'll be here all day."

"I got time."

"Oh sure, *you* got time. But I still have to get to work."

"Relax, Denny. Work is the LEAST of your worries now."

Well, I don't need to tell you I was beginning to shit bricks. Was I sipping my last cup of coffee in this lifetime? What was the guy thinking? Heart attack? Stroke? Maybe an "accident" like a major house fire?

As if hearing my thoughts, he said, "Don't worry, Denny. I'm going to let YOU stew for YEARS! I've got no torments as good as the ones you cook up for yourself. I like to watch."

"Then, what is it? You want a FAVOR or something. You need a hand? You looking for a snitch, or . . . an accomplice, God Forbid?

He winced. No shit, the sonofabitch actually winced and

said, "Please, I'd appreciate it if you left THAT NAME out of this. Believe me, this has nothing to do with HIM."

"Him? Who HIM? Oh, you mean GOD?"

He winced again and I shouted, "GOD! GOD! GOD! GOD! GOD!"

The devil turned black, and the whole house began to tremble as if some ectoplasmic geyser was about to erupt. He clutched the edge of the table as if trying to control himself, and through clenched teeth, he boomed, "ENOUGH ALREADY—you're not hurting me, asshole, but you're really PISSING ME OFF!"

Not a good idea.

"Alright, already! Jesus Christ, can't you take a joke?"

"And now it's Jesus Christ, is it? I'm losing patience with you, Denny. I'm a guest in your house, and you insult me?"

"An UNINVITED guest. What do you expect? It's not like I was expecting you!"

"Denny, you invite me in every day in, oh, so *many* ways. All the little lapses in word and deed. All the little lies of ommission, not to mention the anger, the judgment, the impatience. All the little adulteries in your heart."

"You mean it's TRUE that it's just as bad to *think* about it as it is to *do* it?"

"Ha, wouldn't you like to know."

"Well, I've been meaning to brush up on this good and evil thing. Sometimes it seems so simple, but when I READ about it, I get confused. You know, what with ancient codes, new morality, situation ethics, and what all. . . . I mean even in the Bible . . . in one place Jesus . . . excuse me, I mean, this guy says, 'Whoever is not for me is against me.' And in another place he says, 'Whoever is not against me is on my side.' So where does that leave me? Then it says, 'Thou shalt not kill . . . EXCEPT under certain circumstances and then this guy ORDERS his followers to massacre all their enemies, down to the last child. . . . "

"What makes you think I'm here to discuss such weighty mat-ters—does anyone really care what YOU think about GOOD and EVIL? As for HIM and his overrated scriptures, do you think I was asleep at the switch when all that was going on? I'm surprised that a smart guy like you can't see what a hand I had in all that."

"Are you telling me YOU wrote the Bible?"

"Let's just say I slipped in a few glitches to keep things inter-esting. I love the Fundamentalists. They absolutely fill the halls of hell with damned souls. They just can't believe that HE would allow any misinformation into HIS little rule books. What a joke. HE lets me EXIST, doesn't HE? Anyway, I'm not here to get into anything so profound. My records show that you owe me one, and I'm just stopping by to collect."

"ONE? One what? One soul? One life?"

"No, no, nothing like that. I just need one little SIN. I'm here about Connie's box of deluxe filled chocolates, the one on top of your refrigerator."

"Well, Connie, I don't need to tell you that my heart stopped when he mentioned your chocolates. I already felt guilty about eating so many. Hadn't I done enough? Did he want me to eat them ALL?"

"You're telling me that the DEVIL sat here and talked you into eating all my chocolates?"

"Well, it wasn't so much that he lured me into sin. . . . He said, 'You know Connie is trying to lose weight, Denny.' I should have figured he was behind this drive to diet, even when girls look so GREAT."

"No one needs MY help feeling inadequate, Denny," he said. "Especially you. You've had that one covered since birth. But don't change the subject. You KNOW how Connie is always giv-ing you the unhealthy food she buys. You know how remorseful she is when she gets home with a bag of potato chips or two litres of Coke. . . ."

"Oh, I get it. You're telling me that I'm doing her a FAVOR by scarfing up her chocolate!"

"Oh, not only THAT, Denny. You know how resentful you were that cousin Harold gave those deluxe chocolates to Connie but NOT TO YOU. Think about it. . . . Fair is fair. And it's just a LITTLE sin I asking for, after all."

It was at this moment that I realized that I was talking to the Devil himself, Beelzebub, Old Nick, Satan, Lucifer, THE FATHER OF LIES, and all that. . . .

"So I'm asking you, Connie, to keep an open mind. True is true. And we all know that a really good liar uses truths to gain your confidence. If the DEVIL wanted me to eat those chocolates, wouldn't he tell me NOT TO? Wouldn't the Devil expect you to do the OPPOSITE of what he asked?

"That's why I figured what he really wanted was for me to leave those chocolates alone so they'd be there to lead YOU into sin. You see, by scarfing those chocolates, I actually saved you from temptation and foiled the wily old devil at the same time!"

Connie nodded, blushed, grinned up at me and stirred her coffee with her finger. It steamed, as if the stirring made it hotter. "It's okay, Denny. I understand."

And the house seemed to shake a little.

Painting

PAINTING, LIKE WRITING, can be approached with everything from voluptuous carnality to anguished radiance to fastidious illumination. A painting can be classically representational, sensuously abstract, softly impressionistic, caustically expressionistic, cubistically refracted, playfully trompe l'oeil, even satirically cartoonish. Each stylistic approach conveys an altogether different response to its subject and revelation about the mind of the artist. Likewise, the palette, whether the color is hurled, dripped, rolled, or airbrushed.

"If light and shade imply the understanding of things," John Ruskin wrote, "then color implies the imagination and sentiment of them." Indeed, color—imbued with connotation, history, and inferences of taste—is highly emotional and symbolic. Red, for example, evokes thoughts and images of blood, shame, drama, and royalty. Purple is easily associated with passion and imperial splendor. Yellow and gold intimate radiance, brightness, the sun. Green can be associated, on the one hand, with emerald elegance, and on the other, with putrid decay. In the following example, a student explores interpretations of the color pink:

In the Pink

I'm in the pink, fading into a background of pale pink. Not red. Not bright, exciting red. Red can be frightening—walls of fire, red-hot toughness, spilled blood. In the red means in trouble, debt, despair.

Just pink. In the pink, pale pink, warm center pink. Pink champagne and serendipity dust, rare pink crystal spinning over time, reflecting more than revealing. Diffused light channeled through a pink refracted prism of drawing startling, even painful clarity. Tangled ideas emerge through the pink as brilliant rays of truth, intuitive and clarion. In the pink, their facets glimmer. In the pink, the vision articulates. In the garden, pink flowers grow.

Pink isn't so bad. Pink can pack a punch way beyond that of femininity—a gender tourniquet, soft pink booties, smooth ribbons.

Pink, halfway between red and white is pink, middle, medium, median, average, stable, strong, no longer white. Thorny red roses have drawn blood on white linen paper—pink slips ensue. No longer pure, no longer naive, no longer white. Now pink. Soft, gentle, strong, sturdy, soothing pink. Proud to be pink.

In Living Color

Assignment: Describe a piece of intimate apparel in a color that, normally, you would never wear.

Example: Wait a minute! A red satin bra! Sexy. Silky. Hot. Daring. . . . Confining. I hate bras! That one's pretty, but looks uncomfortable. Maybe for me, because I refuse to be sexy, silky, hot. I used to want it. Now it feels like I've dug my heels in and refuse to budge. What did it ever get me anyway? Guys are the same, no matter what you do, who you are.

Example: Happy Valentine's! I want to buy red bras. I don't need to be in love to do that. But what's my size? I'm a child with breasts. I don't even know my measurements. That's why women think I'm a man on America Online. I never pass the test on the size of the boobs. Only mother and my lovers ever bought me bras. Never myself. That's why I constantly need a full sentimental existence: to fill my closets.

Review: How did the color affect your feeling about the object? Who would you feel like wearing it? What does it feel like to be this person?

Art is at once the specific and the universal. It is the exquisite detail and the vast reference in a single stroke. Art nourishes sensation. It teaches the pleasures of restraint and indulgence, even luxuriance. Art allows the safe surrender to passion.

We Get Not What We Want, but What We Believe: A Demonstration

FOR A GOOD part of my professional career, I worked as a freelance photo stylist for home-design magazines. My job was to walk into a house; make a visual survey of its architecture, furniture, and decorative elements; and recompose the rooms in a way that would tell a specific story for the camera. I loved the work because of the way it exercised my sense of narration and skills at composition.

The last magazine assignment I accepted was one of the most significant of my styling career. It was the kitchen of a multimillion-dollar house, and it was one of the most lavish, overdesigned, poorly decorated, and soulless rooms I'd ever encountered. To my great horror, the homeowner turned out to be a professional kitchen designer—a highly successful one—and had created this kitchen herself!

I noticed, throughout the many hours of the shoot, how the homeowner was continually on the phone with clients. When I remarked at the wide scope of her clientele, she answered simply, "Well, I'm very good at what I do."

I looked around at that kitchen with her words echoing in my ears and recognized the profundity of the message. It didn't matter whether this woman was as visionary as Michelangelo or as blind as a bat, whether she had the decorating sensibilities of Madame de Pompadour or Helen Keller—she *believed* she was great and that the world was yearning for her work. As a result, her practice thrived.

It was that simple. It *is* that simple. We get not what we want, but what we believe, and when we leave no room in our minds for doubt, manifestation—or healing—is inevitable. We may have little or no control over their timing, but with our faith, we lure and anchor them. Healing and manifestation are not the capricious expressions of an external power. They are a result of our inner work.

When I reached the point in my life that I could redevote myself to making art, the work came easily. The years of photo styling, and a lifetime of looking at and writing about art, had given me complete trust in my eyes. My spiritual pursuits had provided understanding of symbolism and meaning. The mastery of this writing process had not only opened me to my subconscious wealth but had also taught me effortless alchemy.

For years I had written, drawn, danced, and prayed for healing. At last I was performing them as acts of celebration. The hope of this book is that your writing leads you to a celebration of your unique life.

Additional Exercises
for Further Work

THE WRITING PROCESS this book teaches is ongoing. You may wish to return to various exercises from time to time. You may also wish to examine other questions. The suggested exercises that follow will lead you through further exploration.

Make a list of people who broke your heart.
Make a list of people whose heart you have broken.
Write about broken hearts.

Make a list of people who have broken promises to you.
Make a list of promises you have broken to others.

Describe the most tight-fisted person you've ever met.
Describe the most generous.
In what aspects of your own personality do you see each reflected?

What do you consider your most unique quality? How do you give it out? How do you sustain or nourish it?

With whom do you most often compare yourself? With whom do you think that person most compares herself or himself?

Describe the happiest day of your life.

You have been transported to a foreign land where no one knows you at all and you can totally reinvent yourself. What is the place and who would you become?

Write about shattered faith.
Make a list of everything you have faith in today.

If you were to start a new religion, what would be its mission? Its rituals? Its belief about the afterlife?
What would its altars, icons, and artifacts look like? Its dress code?

You can have any house, anywhere in the world. What does it look like, feel like, and sound like?

You are part of a group. Describe yourself as its founder, present leader, a follower, dissenter, an exile.

You can wear only one style of clothing—describe this uniform for your life.

You are to give five gifts. Who will you bestow them upon? What are they? How will you present them?

Glossary

THE FOLLOWING DEFINITIONS are based on metaphysical understanding. Their meanings are given here in terms of their application in this book, and in the general philosophy of creativity and healing.

Acceptance   Conscious surrender.

Awareness   The state of conscious aliveness.

Beauty   That which reflects the shape of the soul.

Buddha   One who is awake.

Consciousness   Innate awareness of the divine power that creates, generates, and preserves life.

Crisis   Derives from the Greek *krisis,* meaning "to decide."

Cure   A typically passive process in which symptoms are relieved due to the attentions or ministrations of an external source. Its effect is to successfully control or cause the abatement of the physical progression of a condition without necessarily alleviating the spiritual, emotional, or psychological stresses that produced it.

Depression   A release of energy or life force without consciousness.

Detachment   The nonjudgmental recognition of whatever one has created, promoted, and/or allowed.

Disillusion   The loss of illusion. While disillusion is painful, it can also be highly constructive. With illusions dispelled, truth becomes visible and apprehensible.

Dispel   To relieve attachment to a story in which one is deeply invested.

Energy   The vibrational expression of the life force.

Enthusiasm   Derives from the Greek *enthousiasmos,* meaning "passionate excitement." Vibrant or energetic expression.

Faith   A fertile condition of receptivity to that which the mind does not yet see or comprehend.

Forgiveness   The willingness to see a person or situation from a different point of view. Forgiveness is the generator of miracles.

Grace   An exquisite energy frequency activated by spirit and whose presence and potency are enhanced by liberation from negative attachments.

Healing   An active and internal exploration of beliefs, attitudes, memories, and feelings with the intention of releasing negative patterns of thought and behavior; a return to balance, wholeness, and alignment with divine power. Its effect is increased power for the creation of health, self-esteem, and love.

Health   The physical and psychological state resulting from uninhibited and unimpeded communication among mind, heart, and body.

Incantation   Derives from the Latin *cantare,* meaning "to sing." The words or stories with which we sing a spell into manifestation form an incantation.

Inspiration   Derives from the Latin *spirare,* meaning "to breathe." The essence of the life force is within the breath. To breathe with consciousness of the life force is to be inspired.

Integrity   Derives from the Latin *integer,* meaning "one." To be whole, complete (i.e., one) is to possess integrity.

Intuition   Sensory intelligence.

Luck   The meeting of preparation and opportunity.

Miracle   A shift in perception that creates an opening in the heart/mind and eventually results in manifestation.

Passion   Sustained enthusiasm.

Power   The energy that promotes life and is the foundation for health.

Repentance   Derives from the French *repenser,* meaning "to think again." In a spiritual context, this means to rethink in alignment with divine thought.

Response   Derives from the Latin *responsum,* meaning "to pledge, to promise." Metaphysically, this means to acknowledge a feeling and creatively honor it.

Ritual   An act that calls forth spirit. An act that calls forth and embraces the shadow, putting it to rest.

Sacrifice   Derives from the Latin *sacrare,* meaning "to make sacred."

Shadow   The body of self-knowledge repressed in the subconscious.

Sin   Derives from the archery term meaning "to miss the mark," that is, to think or act in a way that is unaligned with the

Divine and to need repentance, or rethinking in alignment with the Divine.

Suffering   Attachment to pain.

Truth   Consciousness of innate bliss.

Will   The intention to see and accept truths, to explore the subconscious without judgment, and to recognize how one has used one's energies and to be open to redirection.

Recommended Reading

I HEARTILY RECOMMEND any and all of the books written by Julia Cameron, Deepak Chopra, Natalie Goldberg, Caroline Myss, Ph.D., and Andrew Weil as well as the following and in particular:

Bachelard, Gaston. *The Poetics of Reverie*. Boston: Beacon Press, 1971.

————. *The Poetics of Space*. Boston: Beacon Press, 1994.

Barasch, Marc Ian. *The Healing Path*. New York: Penguin Books, 1993.

Borysenko, Joan, Ph.D. *Guilt Is the Teacher, Love Is the Lesson*. New York: Warner Books, 1991.

————. *Minding the Body, Mending the Mind*. New York: Warner Books, 1988.

Bradbury, Ray. *Zen in the Art of Writing: Essays on Creativity*. Capra Press, 1989.

Cameron, Julia. *The Vein of Gold*. New York: Jeremy P. Tacher/Putnam, 1996.

———— and Mark Bryan. *The Artist's Way: A Spiritual Path*

to Higher Creativity. Los Angeles: Jeremy P. Tarcher/ Putnam, 1992.

Cassou, Michelle and Stewart Cubley. *Life, Paint & Passion*. Los Angeles: Jeremy P. Tarcher/Putnam, 1995.

Chopra, Deepak. *The Seven Spiritual Laws of Success*. New York: Amber-Allen Pub., 1995.

A Course in Miracles. Tiburon, CA: Foundation for Inner Peace, 1975, 1985.

Cousins, Norman. *Anatomy of an Illness*. New York: Bantam Books, 1979.

DeMello, Anthony. *Awareness*. New York: Image Books/Doubleday, 1992.

Dillard, Annie. "Write Till You Drop," *The New York Times Book Review*, page 1. 1990.

Edwards, Betty. *Drawing on the Right Side of the Brain*. Los Angeles: Jeremy P. Tarcher/Putnam, 1979.

Estes, Clarissa Pinkola, Ph.D. *Women Who Run with the Wolves*. New York: Ballantine Books, 1997.

Gablik, Suzi. *Conversations Before the End of Time*. London: Thames and Hudson, 1995.

Gawain, Shakti. *Creative Visualization*. Mill Valley, CA: Whatever Publishing, 1978.

Goldberg, Bonni. *Room to Write*. New York: G. P. Putnam's Sons, 1996.

Goldberg, Natalie. *Writing Down the Bones*. Boston: Shambhala Publications, 1986.

————. *Wild Mind: Living the Writer's Life*. New York: Bantam Books, 1990.

Goldberg, Philip. *The Intuitive Edge*. Los Angeles: Jeremy P. Tarcher/Putnam, 1985.

Grudin, Robert. *The Grace of Great Things*. New York: Tickner & Fields, 1991.

Jampolsky, Gerald. *Love Is Letting Go of Fear*. Millbrae, CA: Celestial Arts, 1995.

Jeffers, Susan. *Feel the Fear & Do It Anyway*. New York: Fawcett Columbine, 1997.

Johnson, Robert A. *Ecstasy: Understanding the Psychology of Joy*. San Francisco: HarperCollins, 1989.

————. *Owning Your Own Shadow*. San Francisco: HarperCollins, 1993.

Kandinsky, Wassily. *Concerning the Spiritual in Art*. Dover Books, 1977.

Lamott, Anne. *Bird by Bird*. New York: Anchor, 1995.

Lee, John and Ceci Miller-Kritsberg. *Writing from the Body*. New York: St. Martin's Press, 1994.

McNiff, Shaun. *Art As Medicine*. Boston: Shambhala Publications, 1992.

Metzger, Deena. *Writing for Your Life*. San Francisco: HarperCollins, 1992.

Mindell, Arnold. *The Shaman's Body: A New Shamanism for Transforming Health, Relationships & the Community*. San Francisco: HarperCollins, 1993.

Nachmanovitch, Stephen. *Free Play*. Los Angeles: Jeremy P. Tarcher/Putnam, 1991.

Northrup, Christiane. *Women's Bodies, Women's Wisdom*. New York: Bantam Books, 1994.

Pierrakos, Eva. *Guide Lectures for Self-Transformation*. New York: Center for the Living Force, 1984.

Ram, Dass. *Be Here Now*. N. Mex: Lama Foundation, 1971.

Rico, Gabriele. *Writing the Natural Way*. Los Angeles: Jeremy P. Tarcher/Putnam, 1983.

Sobel, Elliot. *Wild Heart Dancing*. New York: Simon & Schuster, 1994.

Spence, Gerry. *How to Argue & Win Every Time*. New York: St. Martin's, 1995.

Stone, Alan A., M.D. "Where Will Psychoanalysis Survive?" *Harvard Magazine*. Jan.–Feb., 1997, p. 35–39.

Ueland, Brenda. *If You Want to Write*. New York: G. P. Putnam's Sons, 1987.

Walker, Barbara G. *The Woman's Encyclopedia of Myths & Secrets*. Edison, New Jersey: Castle Books, 1996.

Weed, Susan S. *Healing Wise*. Woodstock, NY: Ash Tree Publishing, 1989.

Weil, Andrew, M.D. *Spontaneous Healing: How to Discover & Enhance Your Body's Natural Ability to Maintain & Heal Itself*. New York: Fawcett, 1996

Wooldridge, Susan. *Poem Crazy*. New York: Crown, 1996.

Zukav, Gary. *The Seat of the Soul*. New York: Fireside/Simon & Schuster, 1990.

Index

About the Author

WRITER AND ARTIST Laura Cerwinske considers Creativity to be the highest expression of power and healing. *Writing As a Healing Art: The Transforming Power of Self-Expression* illustrates her belief in passion as an instrument of transformation.

Miss Cerwinske's numerous books on art and design have been published by Rizzoli, Random House, Bantam-Doubleday-Dell, Simon and Schuster, Thames and Hudson, and Pelican Publishing, among others. In addition to earning a degree in fine arts, Miss Cerwinske has studied Byzantine icon painting at the School of Sacred Arts in New York and has worked at the Israel Museum in Jerusalem. She was a gallery reviewer for *Arts* magazine and *The Jerusalem Post*, and the founding editor of *Florida Home and Garden* magazine.

In the course of her thirty-year exploration of spiritual practice and the healing arts, Laura Cerwinske has studied meditation, creative visualization, reiki (laying on of hands), hypnotherapy, and shamanism. She has worked with Reichian therapy; primal therapy; traditional psychotherapy; the Wise Woman tradition of healing; and Santeria, the African Cuban religion derived from the Yoruba tradition of western Nigeria.

Miss Cerwinske's artwork expresses her love of narration, ornament, and spiritual expression. Drawing from Byzantine iconography, medieval manuscript illumination, and various folk traditions, her sculptures and assemblages resemble ritual objects, and icons. They marry precious materials with *objets trouvé*; and rusted surfaces with gilded finishes, creating a look of burnished elegance, an effect of opulent decay. Her present body of work is entitled *The Art of Fulfaggotry: Icons, Altars, and Artifacts from the Worship of the Goddess of Beauty, Creativity, the Extravagant, the Voluptuous, and the Ridiculous.*

In a Spiritual Style, Miss Cerwinske's most recently published book (Thames and Hudson, 1998), begins with a history of worship as it has been expressed in art, architecture, and design. This knowledge also informs her approach to healing and teaching, as *Writing As a Healing Art* amply demonstrates.